UPPITY WOMEN
OF ANCIENT TIMES

UPPITY WOMEN
OF ANCIENT TIMES

BY

VICKI LEÓN

Conari Press
Berkeley, CA

Poetry excerpts are reprinted by the kind permission of the following:

"Enheduana": excerpt from *The Exaltation of Inanna*, by William W. Hallo and J.J.A. Van Dijk, copyright ©1968 by Hallo and Van Dijk. Reprinted by permission of Yale University Press.

"Kubatum": 5 lines from "Shu-Sin's Ritual Bride," from *Women in Praise of the Sacred*, by Jane Hirshfield. copyright ©1994 by Jane Hirshfield. Reprinted by permission of HarperCollins Publishers, Inc.

"Rhodopis": 6 lines from "Her Brother's Mistress," from *Sappho of Lesbos*, by Beram Saklatvala, copyright ©1968 by Beran Saklatvala, Reprinted by permission of Charles Skilton Limited.

"Sulpicia": 7 lines from *The Woman and the Lyre*, by Jane McIntosh Snyder. Translation by Jane McIntosh Snyder. Copyright ©1989 by The Board of Trustees, Southern Illinois University, reprinted with permission of the publisher.

Illustrations and photo credits:
All maps copyright ©1995 by Vicki León and Ashala Lawler.
Author photo: Forrest Doud.
The Bettmann Archive: p.p. 31, 61, 81, 99, 115, 121, 139, 151, 163, 177
Alinari/Art Resource, NY
1. S0048480   AL6509   B&W Print
    Aspasia of Miletus, Vatican Museums, Vatican State. (p. 161)

Conari Press books are distributed by Publishers Group West
Cover: Sharon Smith Design   Cover photo: "Ladies in Blue," Fresco from Knossos (16th century B.C.)

Library of Congress Cataloging-in-Publication Data
Leon, Vicki.
        Uppity women of ancient times/by Vicki Leon
            p. cm.
        Includes bibliographical references and index
        ISBN: 1-57324-010-9 (trade paper)
            1. Women—History—To 500 I. Title
        HQ1127.L46 1995
        305.4'09'01—dc20   95-4886

Printed in the United States of America on recycled paper

10   9   8   7   6   5   4   3

To the uppity women in this book
who have waited so long for their applause;
and to the frisky females in my family
who inspired my search.

OTHER BOOKS IN THIS SERIES:

Wild Women:
Crusaders, Curmudgeons and Completely Corsetless
Ladies in the Otherwise Virtuous Victorian Era
by Autumn Stephens

Untamed Tongues:
Wild Words from Wild Women
by Autumn Stephens

CONTENTS

UPPITY B.C. DEFINED AND DISCOVERED

"A proper name is something living;
its persistence through the centuries shows this vital force."

—Helen Diner, *Mothers & Amazons*

What's in a name, anyway? As trademark lawyers and uppity women will tell you: *everything.* Ancient history specialized in the female put-down by side-step, its accounts being full of "a woman who . . ." and "wife of . . .," not to forget that old favorite, "said to be the mother of. . . ."

And yet, between 2500 B.C. and A.D. 450, throughout Mesopotamia, in Egypt and North Africa, around the Black Sea and the Mediterranean from Britain to the Holy Land, there were countless women who mattered—real-life women, not goddesses or literary figments. Their names have not been lost, just mislaid or glossed over. Most had single monikers such as Kubaba of Kish, Hatshepsut of Egypt, Melanie of Antioch, Gorgo of Sparta, and Fabiola of Rome. Their deeds haven't been lost to us either; uppity women rocked as many cradles as the next gal, but they rocked a lot of boats as well. From different cultures, times, and social classes, they shared a common bond: these high-energy achievers didn't buy into what others said women should and shouldn't do. They knew how to leverage the pluses they were born with—which wasn't much at times. More than a few females in this book were slaves, who often displayed a triumphant sense of self-worth despite their station in life. Like the captive on the auction block who was asked by a picky male shopper in Sparta, "Will you be good if I buy you?" Looking him over, she coolly replied, "Yes—and if you don't buy me as well."

Some uppities chose notoriety over niceness, autonomy over social and sexual conformity. Women like Thecla, the sidekick of Saint Paul, and Artemisia, an admiral from Asia Minor, relished the good fight. Others, like Salome and her murderous mother, Herodias, blithely wallowed in the bad ones. From early Sumer and Egypt into Christian times, women played key roles in spiritual life. On these pages, you'll find the impudent courage of Christian martyrs and the mishaps of Vestal Virgins; whiny teen priestesses, Greek *maenads,* and Hittite wise women; Sumerian poet-priestesses who acted as sacred brides, and Roman matrons who quietly gave millions to the fledgling Christian Church.

On a far from pious note, you'll also hear a lot about the Macedonians from the region north of Greece, to whom the three R's—riding, rubbing out rivals, and running things—were all in a day's work. And you'll encounter a dazzling encyclopedia of women who opted to be poets and poisoners, doctors and gladiators, architects and athletes, money-lenders and big money–spenders, hairdressers and holy terrors, lawyers and litigious homeowners, philosophers and philanderers, supremely saintly wives and sexual supersaleswomen.

All told, this book profiles two hundred women who tackled life on their own terms. Taken as a whole, their lives form a shimmering, surprising look at the common roots, interesting differences, and universal problems of human culture from the female perspective—and their surprising parallels with our own.

Like creating a patchwork quilt from tiny scraps of antique fabric, these women's stories have been winkled out of a vast array of historical and literary sources, often contradictory, hostile, inaccurate, or incomplete—or all of the above. Thankfully, an equally huge body of nonliterary evidence exists. These materials, once called "unconscious sources" by historian Barbara Tuchman, include letters, court cases, artwork, coins, memos, diaries, artifacts, graffiti, and inscriptions. They help give a firsthand feel to ancient life as it really was lived. In some instances, a given picture is still fragmentary—but so is the Venus di Milo, and I don't see anyone throwing out her statue on that account. To give context, each woman's story is woven into a cultural matrix—from the issues that were important to her to the big-picture trends and events of which she may have been a part.

Most of the dates falling within this three-thousand-year span are mushy; as nine out of ten historians would agree, however, meaningful history focuses on links, cultural milestones, and interrelationships—not numbers. Another sticky wicket is the spelling and pronunciation of ancient names. To make this book a delight instead of a multiple-choice ordeal, I've given the commonest and

easiest version of each woman's name. But know that there are many variations out there.

The stage on which these women lived and moved is a huge one. Their civilizations started in the east and south—Mesopotamia and Egypt—and gradually spread west, around the Mediterranean Sea. The hot river valleys of Mesopotamia saw a succession of cultures: Sumer, Akkad, Babylon, Assyria, and Persia. In contrast, Egypt remained Egyptian from earliest times to Cleopatra's day, when it came under the Roman thumb. Asia Minor (present-day Turkey), Syria, and the Holy Land teemed with prosperous cities and kingdoms—often queendoms. The area saw a merry-go-round of cultures and political powers, from Hittites and Phoenicians to Persians, Jews, Greeks, and Romans.

"Greece" was always more concept than country; its regions and city-states never did hang together. When populations grew, city-states sent the surplus to found new colonies around the Mediterranean, which in turn often did the same. These bits and pieces of Greekness kept the world Greek in thought, language, and culture long after it became Roman in a political sense, from 27 B.C. on.

The Roman Empire, on the other hand, let the peoples, regions, and cities under its sway retain their customs. The exception was the Holy Land, where, after much struggle, the Jews were deprived of both religion and real estate. In contrast, the Christian Church, strongly woman-oriented in early centuries, eventually won the hearts and minds of many people, from the Roman empresses on down.

A line from historian Pauline Pantel might well define the ultimate uppity woman B.C.: "Slowly, very slowly, women became individuals, people whose consent mattered." That telling phrase—*people whose consent mattered*—distills what women of long ago fought for and what we, their descendants, continue to claim today. This book is dedicated to every one of those unquenchable and uppity trailblazers and is written in their irreverent spirit.

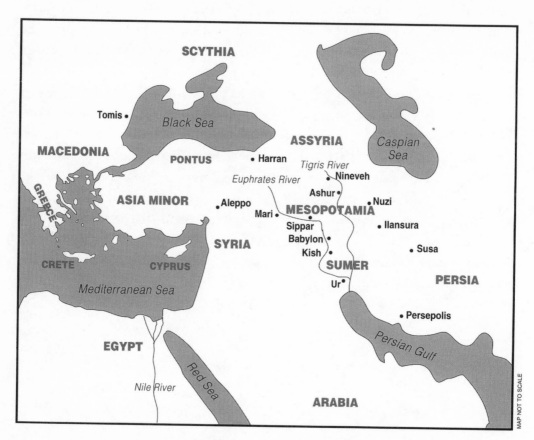

BABYLON & MESOPOTAMIA

SINGERS,
SEXUAL STAND-INS
&
A SASSY SLAVE OR TWO

SHUDI-AD

The 2500 B.C. city of Ur in Sumer was a stylish place, where music, fashion, and the arts flourished at a level of good taste and quality rivaled only by Egypt. Queen Shudi-Ad was one of Ur's patrons, perhaps its inspiration. She and her court lived like, well, kings.

No one has ever worn headgear as exquisite as the Sumerians: delicately original creations of beech leaves and flowers in beaten gold, which must have made the most delightful shimmering effect as they moved. The queen herself wore a tall comb with rosettes of gold, carnelian, and lapis lazuli in her dark wig, and great hoops of gold in her ears. Shudi-Ad drank from goblets of worked gold; her wine was stored in tall jars of veined alabaster. She and her entourage played on gaming boards and musical instruments inlaid with mosaics, and rode in carriages carved with lions and other animals. Even the cylinder seals with which she signed her name were works of art.

But it was music—not only in her circle, but throughout the land of Sumer—that got the most intense attention. Sumerians used the same musical scale we do, and favored harmony and hot licks on the harp, lyre, pipes, and drums. It's easy to imagine their sensual poems being sung; both women and men had honored careers as singers.

As a group, the Sumerians didn't think much of the afterlife. That disbelief, coupled with the absolute power of the ruling class and a very human desire to attend one's own funeral, led them to create the world's first party-and-funeral combination. A pre-death wake, as it were.

Queen Shudi-Ad would have been pleased with her funeral—she was able to enjoy most of it. She was only about forty when she died, of causes unknown but most probably not natural ones. Marching with Shudi-Ad into the grave site, probably accompanied by music, went sixty-four female attendants, half of them wearing gold hair ribbons, the rest silver; an elaborate wooden carriage of gold and silver drawn by two oxen; four female harpists; and six soldiers. (Besides that of Shudi-Ad, archaeologists have found a number of mass burial sites in Sumer; no one really knows why the Sumerians went in for them.)

It appears to have been a cheerful death scene. Everyone was found in perfect repose—not a diadem out of place. The funeral we all fantasize, in fact. Each member of the funeral party was given a drink in a small cup. The harpists played. The singers sang. The crowd might have even done a little karaoke. After all, who would know? And when the music was done and the room became still with her drowsy and dying subjects, I like to think that the beautiful queen gave them a round of applause before she drank down her own cup of nepenthe and lay down in her finery forever.

INNASHAGGA

✿ ✿ ✿ ✿ ✿

The Sumerians loved to go to court, as evidence of their lawsuits, property disputes, and legal grievances shows. One woman whose legal struggles approached the heroic was Innashagga, an ordinary citizen of Sumer forty centuries ago. A shrewd self-starter, she had income of her own with which she bought a house. The records make it clear that this was her property, because Innashagga was married at the time to a fellow named Dudu. (Yes, Dudu—every other Sumerian was named this equivalent of Jason or Michael.)

The couple had a son named Ur-Eninnu; perhaps he was Dudu's son from a former marriage. At any rate (strangely reminiscent of our own times), Dudu's son didn't do doo-doo. You can visualize the exasperated husband saying to his long-suffering wife: "We've got to get this kid out of the house. I know! He can live in your place!" Anything to keep peace in the family; Innashagga let Ur-Eninnu live in her house, even making over the property deed to him. Then Dudu up and died and things got tense. Innashagga owned a male slave called Ninana, given to her by her husband. Upon Dudu's death, the heirs (meaning the slacker son and others) showed up, claiming title to Ninana and the house. They even hauled witnesses and the local priest into court.

Meanwhile ever-resourceful Innashagga got her own witnesses to wail on her behalf, and the court found for her. Not about to give up, the heirs then made a legal claim for Ninana's kids, who were also slaves. Innashagga didn't miss a beat. Before sashaying out of the courtroom, she legally freed Ninana's three daughters, leaving Dudu's would-be heirs undone.

URNANSHE

Music has always been an equal opportunity employer. Like the Greek bard Homer and any number of American music legends, Sumer's greatest singer may have been blind. Known as Ur Nanshe or Ur Nina, she unleashed her creative gifts around 2500 B.C. while living at the court of King Iblul-il in the city-state of Mari (eastern Syria). Located in the desert, Mari was a class venue, from its temple of Ishtar to the 250-room palace where the vocalist probably had her quarters. Ur Nanshe performed both religious favorites and pop standards; besides singing, she played the lyre and danced (you had to be versatile to get gigs in ancient Sumer). They may not have had limos, but Sumer singers were fussed over: Their ailments got special attention at a clinic for warblers, and royal singers got a daily wine ration, which might explain the need for the clinic.

Not having Emmy awards or T-shirts, Sumerians honored their musical celeb in other ways. In their time, seated statues of their superstar, with her signature long black hair and brilliant blue eyes, adorned the temples. Nearly 4,500 years later, these portraits, with their inscriptions that simply say "Ur Nanshe—the Great Singer," have come to light. Now that's fame—Ray and José, eat your hearts out.

KUBABA

The Sumerians, who lived between the muddy rivers of the Tigris and Euphrates in flat, jalapeño-hot Mesopotamia (present-day Iraq), loved order. They were great list-makers, and all that writing seemed to give them a powerful thirst, which they quenched with barley beer. Man, woman, and child, the Sumerians loved their suds. They even had a slogan: "Beer makes the liver happy and fills the heart with joy." There was a reasonable rationale for their enthusiasm. In ancient times, water was likely to make your whole system unhappy. Thick barley beer, on the other hand, was relatively germ-free and nourishing too, even if you did have to drink it through a tube. Religion was big with Sumerians, but the taverns probably saw more of them than the temples. Women dominated the beer cycle: They made most of it, sold most of it, and drank their fair share.

Kubaba, a sharp and sturdy lady who kept a tavern in the Sumerian city of Kish, lived about fifty-five miles south of modern Baghdad. Then as now, taverns had a rep for rowdiness, rigged prices, and watered drinks. Although priestesses got as dry as the next Sumerian, they were forbidden by law to stop by for a cool one. Penalties were a bit stiff: death! Yet as ration lists show, priestesses drank beer daily, so barkeeps probably made beer runs to the temples.

Kubaba herself had higher ambitions than pulling drafts and running the local version of *Cheers*. With the possible help of some beer-oriented campaign promises, she managed to become queen of Kish, gaining the throne about 2500 B.C. (The lack of detail isn't unusual—no one has a clue how Sargon the Great went from his humble origins to a stint as one of Sumer's most famous kings, either.) No splash-in-the-beer-barrel, one-term ruler, Kubaba rose to highest prominence and stayed there. Her sons succeeded her, and the dynasty she founded lasted for one hundred years.

During her tenure, Kubaba "made firm the foundations of Kish." Sounds like earthquake retrofitting, but it may mean she extended political control over other parts of Sumer. But kegmeister Kubaba never forgot her taphouse background. On the official Sumerian kings' list, which has survived to this day, she simply styled herself as "Kubaba the beer woman." In contrast to the "Yo! I'm the greatest!" bombast of most ancient rulers, that's class.

For centuries, the coolest spot (literally and otherwise) in beautiful downtown Babylon was the Hanging Gardens, one of the seven wonders of the ancient world. Queen Semiramis often gets credit for their creation, but like the Taj Mahal, the gardens were built by a man for the love of a woman. **Amytis**, a Mede who married King Nebuchadnezzar and became queen of Babylon, longed for the green hills of home, so the king set about giving her the sixth-century B.C. version of virtual reality. The gardens might have looked like a soft emerald ziggurat, the stepped pyramids Babylonians were good at making. After the burning flatness of Babylon, Amytis probably called its fountains, flowers, and fragrant terraces a piece of paradise.

ENHEDUANA

More than 4,300 years ago, the world's first author to be known by name began her creative work. A poet and priestess, she was the daughter of King Sargon of Akkad, a big name in Sumer's early history.

The small independent cities of Sumer had flat-roofed buildings clustered around a temple complex with a stepped pyramid called a ziggurat. In those distant days, two racial groups jockeyed for position—the Sumerians and the Semites. During Enheduana's life, the Semites ruled, thanks to her dad. A farm boy, Sargon bounced to royal cup-bearer and then to king of Sumer and Akkad. Besides her status as a "Jewish princess" before Jews even existed, Enheduana inherited a lion's share of Dad's ambition and energy. As high priestess to the moon-god Nanna of Ur, she held the top slot, religiously speaking, for more than two decades. Besides prayers and prophesies, the high priestess starred in a drama each spring. On the top floor of the temple where Enheduana lived, she and the current king played bride and groom, reenacting the "sacred marriage" for the continued prosperity of the city.

This sacred marriage rite was tricky; the participants consummated it all right, but only certain bedroom behavior was kosher. (The priestess wasn't supposed to get pregnant, so "kosher" meant anal intercourse and similar strategies.) Once Lugalanne, ruler and high priest of the nearby city of Uruk and Enheduana's brother-in-law, played the groom with far too much enthusiasm. Enheduana later wrote about his behavior and cursed his city to boot. Not a woman to trifle with, sacred marriage or no.

In addition to her priestess duties, Enheduana wrote poetry and prose; her forty-two hymns to the temples of Sumer and Akkad still exist. Besides having poetic merit, they help explain Sumerian theological beliefs. Her poems were highly popular, both in her time and later. Fifty clay "reprints" of one of her poems have been found—nearly twice the number discovered of other better-known hymns.

After her father died, Enheduana's clueless twin brothers took turns on the throne, followed by her nasty nephew Naram-Sin, who chucked her out of office—boom! no benefits, no nothing—and installed his own daughter as high priestess. Undismayed, Enheduana used her ouster as raw material for her work, proving once again that the pen is mightier than the pink slip:

> *(Me) who once sat triumphant, he has driven out of the sanctuary.*
> *Like a swallow he made me fly from the window,*
> *My life is consumed.*
> *He stripped me of the crown appropriate for the high priesthood.*
> *He gave me dagger and sword—"it becomes you," he said to me.*

KUBATUM

After plowing through endless verses of "A begat B," the Song of Solomon in the Old Testament comes as a shock. Generations of readers have wondered: Spiritual love, my foot—where'd this hot stuff come from? The answer now seems to be from Sumer. Although Sumerians invented cuneiform writing to make list-making easier, they soon got down to more exciting topics, such as sex and love. A favorite was their myth of Dumuzi, a human shepherd who fell for the moon-goddess Inanna and won her heart and bed. Even scholars use words like *erotic enthusiasm* to describe their religious literature.

Kubatum, a priestess in the city of Ur around 2030 B.C., relived the myth and wrote about it. Each spring at the Sumerian New Year, she and the reigning king did an instant replay of the Sacred Marriage of Dumuzi and Inanna, to guarantee that both crops and locals would prosper. Kubatum became a special favorite of King Shu-Sin; perhaps she reminded him of his grandmother Abisimti, a dynamic woman who helped rule Ur for forty-seven years and lived to age eighty. Shu-Sin laid beautiful jewelry on Kubatum and evidently spent quite a bit more than the regulation one hot night per year in her bed atop the multistory temple.

In turn, besides erotic enthusiasm, Kubatum gave him immortality. She wrote several marriage songs about the ritual courtship they shared, whose rhythms, theme, and imagery were generously borrowed from by later Hebrew writers to compose the Song of Solomon. Here's a typical morsel of Kubatum's verse:

My sweet one, wash me with honey—
In the bed that is filled with honey,
Let us enjoy our love.
Lion, let me give you my caresses,
My sweet one, wash me with honey.

Although the honey-filled bed may sound like a dry-cleaning nightmare, poet Kubatum was clearly a woman who knew what she wanted; milk and honey references are standard sexual euphemisms in Near Eastern love poetry.

AMAT-MAMU

Ever tried to take an inventory verbally? That hassle motivated the Sumerians to invent writing, which grew into a six-hundred-symbol language called cuneiform. Because they used wet clay as their "paper," huge numbers of their laundry lists, curses, legal briefs, school papers, personal letters, and love songs exist on dry clay tablets today.

As writing became hip, so did the profession of scribe. Becoming a scribe was the B.C. equivalent of law school: costly, slow, and male dominated. Women had to be from a scribal family or the upper class to elbow in, as well as motivated to attend classes from sunrise to sunset. Besides writing and reading, pupils learned arithmetic, geometry, and higher math. Part of the scribal gig was to measure things; they did surveying, divided up estates, and arbitrated between parties, especially in property and legal matters.

Amat-Mamu was a career scribe; her forty-year tenure spanned the reign of King Hammurabi—he of the Code of Laws—so we're talking seventeenth century B.C. She lived and worked in a cloister of priestesses in Sippar, an important city and religious center about forty miles from Babylon. Nothing backwoods about her convent: More than 140 priestesses lived there, plus supervisors, slaves, janitors, scribes, cooks, and various "wardens." Sounds like a tough joint to break out of, but convent life was pretty laid-back. The priestesses, many from high-society families, could come and go freely. A few were even married. None, however, were allowed to have kids—Sumerians had "surrogate moms" (usually a concubine or the priestess' sister) for that function.

Far from being unworldly, priestesses transacted much of the city's business. As landowners, they handled property management, bought and sold slaves, and were active in legal matters. Who do you suppose was the backbone of this feverish activity? Amat-Mamu and her crew, of course. To the Sumerian mind, if it ain't down on clay, it doesn't exist. Almost everything we think of as "administration" passed through her busy hands: the temple records, for example, including what was sacrificed to the sun-god Shamash, when, and by whom. (Religious centers accumulated goods and property at an astonishing clip.) In her long career, Amat-Mamu probably came to oversee the work of the other scribes; at this temple, they all seem to have been women. Amat-Mamu didn't know it at the time, but she was leaving us a treasure—most of what we know about Mesopotamian women comes from the life work of Amat-Mamu and her fellow scribes.

SHIBTU

Now it can be told: the interoffice memo was born more than a million days ago in Mari, a luxury city on the upper Euphrates River. This early kingdom in the land of Sumer was famous for quality carpets, wooden carts, superb singers, pomegranate-flavored beer—and putting it in writing. Queen for twenty years and one of Mari's star communicators, Shibtu and her husband Zimri-Lim left a mountain of love letters, personnel files, and memos on clay, giving an intimate and vivid look at their lives. Originally from Aleppo (present-day Syria), at that time the area powerhouse, Shibtu was a king's daughter. She married Zimri-Lim as a political alliance, after which her dad helped her new husband kick the Assyrians out of Mari. Arranged marriage or not, Shibtu and Zimri-Lim clearly lucked out and came to have what we call chemistry, both physical and intellectual.

To hold his newly won country, Zimri-Lim spent a lot of time on the road, glad-handing and stroking allies, taking names and kicking butt where needed. Back at the palace, Shibtu became his right-hand woman, personal deputy, political confidante, and adviser. The two communicated almost incessantly via letters. No palace-bound royal, Shibtu occasionally rendezvoused with him in other cities, a business-with-pleasure strategy that may have kept maximum sizzle in their marriage.

The couple had twins and as many as ten daughters, but megamotherhood didn't slow Shibtu. A horde of officials reported to her in person and by mail or memo. Shibtu also dealt with the fan mail chores, the "I had a bad omen dream" letters, the begging correspondence, and the whiny notes from her children as they grew to adulthood—sort of. When finished for the day, however, Shibtu couldn't just kick back and suck down iced red wine coolers (another Mari specialty); she had more work, overseeing activities in the palace complex. Its hundreds of rooms, warehouses, and courtyards held production centers for textiles, leather, and other luxury goods; a retail market; tax collection quarters; loading docks and storage for goods imported and exported; a scribal school; a temple; residential quarters for the royal family and the palace employees; plus the weather-god only knew how many rooms to hold the document overload. Shibtu's agenda also included making work assignments for royal captives; security arrangements; doing inventories; and coping with personnel problems, such as with Ama-dugga, her truculent housekeeper. And she still found time to make little gifts for Zimmy and the kids.

Shibtu and Zimri-Lim built a wonderful life for themselves and Mari; for decades, their industry and diplomacy kept at bay the aggression that was moving like a tornado through the land, led by King Hammurabi of Babylon. One by one, however, Hammurabi knocked out his rivals, finally taking Mari—the only place barring his way to the Mediterranean—in 1695 B.C. Two years later, he hammered this beautiful city, so full of art and life, into dust—overlooking what is now its biggest treasure: the clay tablets that bring Shibtu and her family to life for us.

KIRU

Although Kiru lived more than 3,700 years ago in northern Mesopotamia, her story is a modern-sounding tale of career versus marriage, sibling rivalry, and spousal abuse, involving herself, her probable half-sister Sibatum, and their probable time-share husband, Haya-Sumu.

Politically speaking, the land of Sumer was never what we would call a country. Instead, a number of small kingdoms or city-states jockeyed for power. Larger city-states, such as Mari, were run by kings or queens; smaller ones, often tribute-paying subjects of the larger ones, were governed by mayors. These mayors didn't make campaign promises or kiss a single baby to get into office—mayorship was by appointment.

Around 1715 B.C., Kiru, one of the ten or so daughters of Queen Shibtu and King Zimri-Lim of Mari, married the king of Ilansura, a two-bit place far from Mari. This was a political marriage, not a love match—nothing unusual for the times. But Kiru's father also appointed her mayor of Ilansura, giving her authority to act and sometimes to overrule her husband, the king.

Both a political realist and a humanist, Zimri-Lim believed that women had brains and should use them. (His relationship with his wife Shibtu, his daughters, and other women in his life show that he was quite a feminist for his era.) Kiru's new husband, on the other hand, was your average Mesopotamian "no way is my wife gonna be my boss" kind of guy. Conflict and heartbreak were just up the road.

Although experts still disagree over the interpretation of Kiru's letters, it appears that as mayor she was competent, influential, and kept her father abreast of the political situation in Ilansura and the north. However, the dad-and-daughter partisanship (and the snitching) really got her husband's goat. At one point, Kiru wrote her dad about a fight they'd had: "Haya-Sumu got right up in my face and said, 'So what if you run things as mayor! I'm going to kill you, so you'd better ask that daddy of yours, your "star," to come and get you!'" Kiru pleaded to be allowed to return to Mari.

What with the power issues between Kiru and her husband, things got sticky, and her sister (or half-sister) Sibatum, who lived with the two, made things worse. The unhappier Kiru got, the more smug Sibatum became. The records imply that Sibatum was also a wife of Haya-Sumu, but lower in rank. Now she was movin' on up, craftily playing the innocent to her harassed father Zimri-Lim: "Why are they always accusing me and slandering me to you? It's all lies, Pop!"

Eventually, Kiru got her wish. She returned to Mari, at the expense of her marriage and her position of authority. And Sibatum? Shrewd in her own way as Zimri-Lim's other daughters, her tactics may have gained her the top marital slot with Haya-Sumu. But not—it's a pretty safe guess—the mayorship.

ERISTI-AYA

Phones hadn't been invented in Sumer in the seventeenth century B.C., but spoiled teens and "Dear Mom and Dad—I need money" letters surely had. Queen Shibtu and King Zimri-Lim of Mari no doubt winced to get the following note, one of many from their priestess daughter Eristi-Aya:

"Aren't I your personal representative to the gods? Don't I constantly pray for your life? So why am I not getting my allowances of oil and honey?"

Eristi-Aya was nudged or forced by her parents to become a naditum priestess. Drawn from the ranks of royalty or wealth, these priestesses lived in convents associated with a given temple. As religious go-betweens, their job was to pray for their fathers and benefactors to the Sumerian gods and goddesses. In Sumer, only women held this job. Perhaps it was politically expedient to have a princess at the important temple of Shamash (the sun god) and Aya (his wife) in Sippar. Or, judging by the tone of her letters, Eristi-Aya may just have been a royal pain in the palace. At any rate, her parents sent her to the temple at Sippar on the Euphrates, conveniently located many miles away, downriver from Mari.

There she settled in to live with other young women in the huge complex. In addition to a little light praying, the nadiatum priestesses did occasional prophesying. What they didn't do was housework, cook, or make clothes. For the real work, the cloister swarmed with servants, most of them female slaves. Each priestess had at least one servant; Eristi-Aya clearly had more. It was no picnic to work for her; in yet another letter home, she says to her father: "I am always crying out, always! Last year you sent me two female slaves, and one of them had to go and die! Now they've brought me two more, and one of those had to go and die!"

Dramatic little thing—the reality of her life was quite plush. She came to the cloister with a nice wardrobe and her own dowry money, just as a daughter getting married would do. Priestesses could come and go from the convent, shopping for perfume and swanky jewelry, which they paid for by snipping off a piece of silver from a silver ring they carried.

Just answering Eristi-Aya's mail, to say nothing of maintaining the flow of oil and honey and humanpower, kept Queen Shibtu and King Zimri-Lim hopping. (Their only stroke of luck was that credit cards and shopping malls hadn't arrived on the scene yet.) Despite the intimacy of her letters, we don't actually know Eristi-Aya's birth name. When she entered the cloister, she took one of the generic priestess names. As time went on, Eristi-Aya, meaning "Request from Aya," must have come to seem grimly appropriate.

KISAYA

Adoption in the ancient Near East wasn't necessarily about kids. Many people adopted adults, especially young females. Originally, the idea was a pretty good one: "Since I'm childless and you're poor, I'll adopt you to be my heir." To make it win-win all around, the adopting parent had to give a cash down payment to the biological parents. In turn, the newly adopted was expected to care for his or her adoptive parent(s) later on down the road, instead of chucking them into the local version of a nursing home. But you know human nature. Sometimes adoption became a euphemism for lifelong slavery.

Such was the case with Kisaya, a young woman of Nuzi, a city-state in northeast Sumer. In mid-fifteenth-century B.C., she was adopted by Tulpunnaya, a local woman already well-known by the long-suffering Nuzian courts for her involvement in legal disputes. Too late, Kisaya got the message: Tulpunnaya was a "mother" all right, but the wrong kind. So she ran away, was tracked down, and sued. Not arrested—sued. That's how the Sumerians did things. Tulpunnaya slapped a suit on her, and Kisaya had to return home. The mother of all schemers then thought: Why not use the obviously too uppity Kisaya to breed kids? So she chose a husband for her, a fellow called Mannuya. Kisaya, meanwhile, had fallen in love with a man named Arteya, and wanted to marry and live life on her own terms. To do so, Kisaya now took Tulpunnaya to court. (Lawyers hadn't evolved yet, so it probably cost less to do this than you think.) What's more, she won her case, and in the presence of seven witnesses, Kisaya and Arteya were married.

But Kisaya paid top dollar for love and freedom of action. The final document in the now-voluminous Kisaya file reads: "I have now given my son Inziteshup, whose father is Arteya, to Tulpunnaya." Fourteen witnesses and seven seals were required to validate this heartbreaking contract, which was put into its clay envelope and carefully sealed with the hem of Kisaya's dress. She then handed over her new baby to the triumphant Tulpunnaya.

Although it's a stretch to think of hard-nosed Tulpunnaya as a role model, she seemed to have been just that for Chanate, a slave of hers. Over the years, Chanate acquired a nest egg by working an outside job, probably as a weaver or dressmaker, where she got to keep some of her wages. To grow her funds further, Chanate adopted a daughter as well. Shades of déjà vu: Her daughter also ran away, was returned by the court, and was made to marry a slave. This postscript to Kisaya's tale is interesting for more than its sad echo. No matter how brutal certain aspects of their lives were, slaves in Sumer at that time had a surprising number of legal rights, from entering into contracts to owning their own slaves.

KIYA

❀ ❀ ❀ ❀ ❀

The glittering but inconsequential King Tut (Tutankhamen of Egypt's eighteenth dynasty, 1334-1325 B.C.) has gotten more than his fifteen minutes of fame. But how about his mother? Who was she, anyway? Until recently, it appeared that young Tut, barely eighteen at death, was the son of unorthodox pharaoh Akhenaten and his dazzling wife, Nefertiti, who hasn't done so badly in the press-adulation category herself. Royal family trees in Egypt being incestuous to the point of overload, it's small wonder that questions remain. But a much more likely candidate for Tut's mom exists, one whose story is just as deserving of its quarter hour.

Her birth name was Tudukhepa, the royal daughter of King Tushratta, who hailed from the kingdom of the Mittanis, far from Egypt's borders in Mesopotamia. A mysterious people, the Mitannis—details about their culture remain few. A horse-mad society, they used war chariots in their struggles with Egypt over Syria, the buffer country the two nations both coveted.

Tudukhepa's life coincided with the Amarna age in Egypt, when religion, culture, and the arts were shaken to the core. The co-shakers were Nefertiti and Akhenaten, both brilliant dreamers who wanted to introduce the worship of one god—and slyly cut back on the swollen power of the long-entrenched priesthood of Amon. This couple really loved family life; they and their six daughters are the most depicted family group in history. Nowhere does a son appear. If Tut were theirs, we would have seen his baby pictures by now.

At the time Tudukhepa was growing up, the Mitannis enjoyed cordial relations with the Egyptians, who had moved their capital from Thebes to Amarna.

To cement their détente, the two kings decided to link Tudukhepa with Akhenaten. (Most kings appreciated their daughters more than nonroyal fathers did; political/sexual alliances were handy, and so useful for job security.) Tudukhepa set out for Egypt, accompanied by her father, wedding gifts such as rare musical instruments, and an entourage that would put a rock star to shame. Although Akhenaten was already married to a real looker (and other women), Tudukhepa captured at least a piece of his heart. Instead of stashing her in the secondary wives' quarters after the ceremony, she became one of his favorites. He gave her the Egyptian name Kiya, and titles such as "Greatly Beloved Wife." Many artifacts with her hieroglyph on them have turned up.

In due course, Kiya had a daughter; the two appear on Amarna wall reliefs. But events took a tragic turn during the eleventh year of the pharaoh's reign: Kiya disappeared. It's now believed that she died giving birth to a second child, the golden boy who would himself die so young.

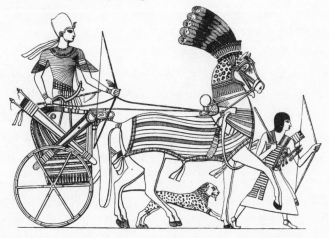

SEMIRAMIS

Uppity women often get accused of "wearing the pants in the family," which seems only right, since trousers were probably invented by a female head of household 2,800 years ago—a woman named Semiramis. Initially, Semiramis had bigger fish to fry than making fashion statements.

Born a Chaldean princess, she caught the biggest fish in the pond with her marriage to King Shamsi-Adad Five of Assyria. This took place in the ninth century B.C., when the military might of the Assyrians had most of Mesopotamia in its grip. The queen's own mojo really got to working when Shamsi-Adad died around 812 B.C., however, and she took the throne for her boy Adad-Nirari.

Under her leadership, a new system of canals and dikes irrigated the flatland between the Tigris and Euphrates Rivers, and the twin cities of Nimrud and Nineveh became the bright lights of Assyria. A true power player, Semiramis led military expeditions against the Medes as far afield as India, and forged tactical alliances as far west as Turkey.

On one of her expeditions—maybe the road-building she did from chilly northern Iran to the Zagros mountains—she came up with the pants prototype, her idea being that they made it harder to tell women from men. As camouflage or to ward off cold, pants became a fashion item—but it was the males who were mad for them. (Not that many women galloped about the icy countryside leading armies, so it took quite a while before gals took to pants again.)

Ancient writers also "credit" Semiramis with introducing eunuchs, or castrated males, into the Assyrian bureaucracy. Not merely fat guys guarding harems, eunuchs were career types—civil servants, high priests, upper-echelon palace staff. Since eunuchs appear in earlier biblical references, it's clear she didn't invent the concept, though she may have made it more widespread. Why on Earth did Semiramis and other royals favor eunuchs? They believed that eunuchs (having no offspring or wives) were more dedicated to their work—tailor-made for the job, you might say.

Although often described as bright and courageous, Semiramis also got bad press, being accused of using men like Kleenexes, as well as of having a thing for her own son. One writer even had her invent a male chas-

Trousers? Yes. Chastity belts? No way.

tity belt—to keep other women away from sonny while she was in battle! This engineering feat can safely be added to the long list of miracles and sexy gossip that attached itself to Semiramis' life in later centuries. At Ashur, the capital, her royal monument still stands among those of the Assyrian kings. If she were abusive or even incompetent, her son would have erased any traces of Semiramis; he was, after all, an unsentimental Assyrian too.

NA'QIA

❀ ❀ ❀ ❀ ❀

Even amid the nonstop pillaging, plotting, and bragging of the Assyrian kings, Na'qia more than held her own as a queenly schemer of Mesopotamian times. Born in Canaan, Na'qia may have arrived at Sennacherib's court in Nineveh as a small cog—a concubine or a political pawn—but not for long. Soon she had Sennacherib, one of Assyria's cruelest kings, purring at her feet. After they married, she moved from second-string to main flame. (His harem remained intact, of course. Marital alliances, foreign wives, and kingly polygamy were the glue of diplomacy in Mesopotamia as elsewhere.)

Together Na'qia and Sennacherib transformed the capital into a major tourist destination on the Tigris River, crowned with an eighty-room split-level which was modestly referred to as The Palace Without Rival. This building project occupied the king's more cherubic moments. Most of the twenty-three years of his reign, Sennacherib roared around the fertile crescent, whipping the Babylonians, the Phoenicians, and the Philistines, followed by a siege of Jerusalem and a second sack of Babylon for good measure.

During his absence on military campaigns, Na'qia acted as de facto ruler. Even though Sennacherib had older sons by another wife, Na'qia was able to talk him into making her son the heir. To no one's astonishment, when their son Esarhaddon was old enough to aim straight, he killed his father, with her encouragement. Sonny's blatant throne-jumping created quite a stink with the older siblings, but Esarhaddon bloodily squelched their rebellion.

With Na'qia's help, the new king rebuilt Babylon, still squashed flat after Sennacherib's kind attentions. By now, Na'qia had grandsons, one of whom was given Babylon to run. But Grandma's favorite was little Ashurbanipal, the younger grandson, supposedly destined for the priesthood. After his father was killed on a campaign in Egypt, he grabbed the throne in 669 B.C. with Granny's help. Older brother Shamash-shum-Ukin plotted to kill Ashurbanipal, but the wily Na'qia sniffed out his plans and it was so long, Shamash.

With this much political moxie and energy, why didn't Na'qia grab the gold ring herself? It's one of history's minor mysteries—especially since the prior century had seen a famous female precedent—Semiramis, the only woman to seat herself on the throne of Assyrian kings.

ASHURSHARRAT

The Assyrians borrowed most of their culture—not that they had much—from the Babylonians and Sumerians. They did shine at one thing: cruelty. Military to the max, they invented puppet states, genocide, and ingenious forms of punishment by mutilation. By the time Queen Ashursharrat and King Ashurbanipal came into power in 668 B.C., their empire sprawled from Syria to Russia.

A typical Assyrian, Ashursharrat had a strong stomach. She and the king used to eat locust and honey dip in a garden whose trees were decorated with trophies of newly severed heads. The one thing she couldn't stomach was her husband's cross-dressing. This mucho macho warrior liked women's duds—more comfy, he said. (Not that anyone asked—unless they were suicidal.) In general, Assyrian males favored chunky jewelry and perfumed beards glued into curls, but Ash went overboard, using cosmetics on his face and body and imitating a woman's voice while talking.

Famed for creating the world's first great library, his reign was the last act of the Assyrian Empire. Shortly before it fell, one story has it that Ashurbanipal prepared a funeral pyre, loaded it with his favorite perfumes, and climbed on board with Ashursharrat and all his wives. Version B says that Ashurbanipal was penciling his eyebrows when one of his generals happened to walk in on him. Disgusted—or perhaps envious—he stabbed the king on the spot.

ADAD-GUPPI

Sometimes a ninety-year life span is just too much. Take Adad-Guppi, who saw the Jews arrive in Babylon to begin their exile; the golden age of the city and builder-king Nebuchadnezzar; and ultimately the swan song of local rule in Mesopotamia, presided over by her equally inept son and grandson. She originally hailed from Harran, a northern city famed for its devotion to the moon-god Sin. A priestess by trade, she raised her son Nabonidus as a devout follower. The two ended up in Babylon, the Big Apple of its day, where Adad-Guppi got her gumptionless son a good job at court. In 555 B.C., now in his sixties, Nabonidus finally became king. Good at restoring things, he had no knack for politics. Worse, he left Babylon in the hands of his son Belshazzar, popular as the plague, while he holed up in the desert for a decade. (By now his mom was wringing her hands.) From time to time, Babylon got a break; when military duties called Belshazzar away, Grandma Guppi probably sat in to run things. But Nabonidus' real political downfall stemmed from his piety. He tried to set up good old Harran moon-god worship in Babylon while slashing funds to the priests of Marduk, the chief god of the city. This recipe for disaster made it a snap for Cyrus the Persian king to work from within; in 539 B.C., he took the city without bloodshed. Adad-Guppi didn't live to see this final downer; she died in about 547 B.C., and was buried in Harran with queen's honors.

ENNIGALDI

Not many women today will achieve three careers in one lifetime; fewer still did so in old Babylonia. In the middle of the sixth century B.C., however, Ennigaldi-Nanna of Ur managed to squeeze in three diverse careers: museum curator, school administrator, and high priestess. Talk about fast track!

Ennigaldi began her life simply as the beloved daughter of Nabonidus, the last home-grown king of Babylon and Ur before the Persians took over. Most Babylonian kings went in for blood sports like war and lion-hunting, activities that translated well onto heroic murals. A few kings, like Nabonidus, had a contemplative side. An antiquarian and restorer, he loved messing about with old things and taught Ennigaldi to appreciate them, too.

When archaeologists excavated certain parts of the palace and temple complex at Ur, they were puzzled to find dozens of artifacts, neatly arranged side by side, whose ages varied by hundreds of years. Then clay drums with labels in three languages showed up—the first known museum labels. They speculated that Ennigaldi and her father may have personally excavated some of the pieces in the museum she maintained—artifacts which were already antiquities in her day.

This museum curator miss found it possible to handle more than one job because she lacked one thing: a commute. The palace grounds included the temple and its ancillary buildings, plus living quarters, the museum building, and a school for priestesses, run by—and possibly taught by—Ennigaldi. By her time, this school had been in continuous operation in the same spot for 845 years. The equipment and teaching techniques at her school resembled other scribal schools—although with young priestesses as students, there may have been less emphasis on the daily canings and other corporal punishment that formed part of the normal Sumerian school curriculum.

Just as male literacy was pretty much reserved for the upper classes, female literacy in Mesopotamia followed the same pattern. Literate women even had their own written dialect, called Emesal. Because of this dialect, archaeologists can tell when women wrote—or were written to—on the tablets.

In 547 B.C., Ennigaldi-Nanna became a high priestess, as her recently deceased grandmother Adad-Guppi had been. Nanna was a male god, the equivalent of the moon-god Sin. So she was a priestess of Sin, which isn't as juicy as it sounds. (With all this work, does it seem likely she'd have much time or inclination?) Ennigaldi now spent nights of religious significance to the moon-god in the small blue room on top of the great ziggurat of Ur.

When Babylonians talked about the mail, they didn't say, "Did you get my letter?" Instead, they asked, "Did you hear my tablet?" We have yet to hear any tablets from Ennigaldi-Nanna; perhaps tomorrow's spade will unearth some direct words from this dynamo of ancient Ur.

TOMYRIS

By 550 B.C., King Cyrus the Great of Persia had hacked a humongous empire from the Mediterranean Sea to India, and his winning streak got him to believing his own PR. After whipping the Assyrians, he looked around for an even badder opponent. Everyone agreed: That would be the Massagetae, nomads of Scythian stock who lived between the Araxes River and the Caspian Sea. Their leader, Tomyris, ruled as queen and commander-in-chief of the fearsome Massagetan army with her grown son, Spargapises, as second in command.

At first, Cyrus figured the widowed Tomyris for a sap. He camped his army at the river and sent her a marriage proposal. All the while, his troops were busy building bridges across the water. Knowing the Persian king was hot to possess her lands and not her body, Tomyris responded with acid politeness: "Cyrus, my advice is to forget about the Massagetae—just rule your own people and try to handle the sight of me ruling mine." She countered by suggesting that both armies retreat from the river while the leaders met to negotiate.

Cyrus and his officers leaned toward the idea, but not so old buddy and vassal Croesus, a filthy rich king of Asia Minor who had already gotten thumped by the Persians. He played the deadly "male wimp" card: "You're talking disgrace here, Cyrus, to give ground to a woman." Croesus proposed a trap: Set up camp on enemy territory and bait it with a few feeble troops and a banquet of food and potent Persian wine for the Massagetan boys, who were known to eat anything and were unused to alcohol. (At nomad parties, they threw a type of fruit into the fire whose smoke supposedly gave them a contact high.)

Tomyris assigned a third of her troops to her son, who fell on the camp, slaughtered the Persians, and attacked the bait, soon becoming sated and drunk. It was then a piece of cake for Cyrus' troops to kill them and take the son prisoner. When word reached Tomyris, she fired off another note: "Cheap shot, Cyrus. Return my son and get out of my country—or I swear I'll give you more blood than even you can drink." Back in the Persian camp, Tomyris' son asked to have his bonds taken off. Before they knew it, the kid had committed suicide. Now his mom had even more reason to be steamed.

With Tomyris at its head, the Massagetae took on Cyrus' larger army, first with bows and arrows, then fighting hand-to-hand with bronze spears and daggers. By the end of one of the most violent battles the world had yet seen, more than 200,000 Persians, including Cyrus, lay dead. At the conclusion of that long and bloody day, Tomyris' troops looked for the king's body. When they came up to her with the corpse, Tomyris filled a goatskin with human blood. Pushing his head contemptuously into it, she said, "Still thirsty for Scythian blood, Cyrus? Go on—drink your fill!"

ATOSSA

A superstar's kid, Atossa was the daughter of Persian megamonarch Cyrus, who was called "the Great" even after being killed in battle by a woman, the Scythian warrior queen Tomyris. (How'd his PR people turn *that* around, I wonder.)

Like the Egyptians, the Persians thought nothing of brother-sister marriages and other interestingly incestuous alliances. A cover-all-bases kind of gal, Atossa first married her drunken brother Cambyses Two, who became king when Daddy took a dive. That marital bout was followed by a mininuptial with a royal wanna-be who styled himself the pseudo-Smerdis. When heads rolled again, as they did with distressing frequency in the Persian succession sweepstakes, Atossa married her other brother, Darius.

Soon after marriage three, the queen got a growth on her breast, which abscessed and spread until she was seriously ill; their on-call physician, a Greek captive, guaranteed a cure—but only if she'd talk her husband into letting him return home. The doc did the trick, so Atossa reciprocated by convincing Darius to send a spy mission with the good doctor as guide.

Now with a new lease on life, Atossa as co-regent helped Darius rule for thirty-five years. They built Susa, the new capital of what was once Babylonia, and a jazzy palace at Persepolis, on a site to die for. In royal politics, Atossa came to have the pivotal vote on who would succeed Darius—and chose her oldest son Xerxes. She might not have done him any favors: Xerxes (even with his reputed 2.6 million troops) went down to mortifyingly major defeat in the Greek-Persian War of 480-479 B.C.

HYPSICRATEA

Talk about an ingrate for a life partner—Hypsicratea sure knew how to pick 'em. A golden-haired sweetheart, she hooked up with high-strung Mithridates the Great around 120 B.C. Their Persian kingdom of Pontus almost circled the Black Sea, but Mr. M. wanted more; he just knew he could whip the Romans, given enough time, money, and bodies. Unlike those stay-at-home queens, Hypsicratea wanted to go places with her man. Granted, she would have preferred a nice time-share, but into battle it was. At least it offered a break from her five sons. War being hell on clothes, Hypsicratea cut her hair, put on helmet and greaves, and splashed *l'eau de* armor rust on her face. Instead of a purse, she lugged a shield and lance.

Besides making love and war, Mithridates' other hobby was poison. He loved to field-test toxins on criminals, taking weaker doses himself to develop antidotes. After fifty-seven hectic years, he had tons of enemies, including a son (he'd offed the other four). As the Romans won back their lands, Hypsicratea suffered with her man, hiding in caves, being chased through Armenia, finally cornered in their own palace by their crabby kid. As reward for schlepping around in the mud for untold years, Hypsicratea got a hit of Love Poison Number Nine from her hubby. The miserable Mr. M. had to exit by way of the blade, since he got no more punch from poisons.

The Romans ended up with Mithridates' antidote recipe. Years later, Nero's doctor added viper flesh and upped the opium content 500 percent to create *theriac*, the world's most popular all-purpose drug of the first few centuries A.D.

VASHTI

❁ ❁ ❁ ❁ ❁

Other than having the absolute power of life and death over every human being from India to Ethiopia, King "Long Hand" Artaxerxes of Persia was a regular guy. He loved hanging out with his male friends and drinking smooth local wine. But most of all, he loved his dishy wife, Vashti, a simply stunning woman from one of the seven bluest-blooded families in Persia.

In the third year of his reign, Artaxerxes spent six months holding an assembly to show off the winter palace at Susa and its *chatchkas* to the vassals of his 127 provinces. The formalities over, he pitched a gold tent for 10,000 and began a banquet for his tight pals, where the wine flowed nonstop into those gold goblets. After a week of partying, Long Hand got one of those ideas that probably seemed fun at the time: He would summon his gorgeous wife and show her off. So he sent in a eunuch or two to give Vashti the message.

He hadn't reckoned on a queen with attitude. A command appearance in front of 10,000 drunken louts was insult enough, but she had the feeling that the king wanted to display *all* her charms. (Persian law was on her side, too: Even the merest squint by a strange male at anyone's wife, to say nothing of the first lady, was taboo.) In any event, Vashti said, "No way!"

The king got hot, but to no avail. He sent in more eunuchs to plead prettyplease. Vashti, however, wouldn't budge from her lavish quarters, where she had a feast and a no-host bar going for her own women friends. Needless to say, the party went downhill from there. A highly irritated Artaxerxes huddled with his top legal beagles, who told him to nip this disobedience thing in the bud. Much as he hated to, he quickly kicked out a memo to everyone in the empire, saying that Vashti was *hasta la vista*. His counselors were more worried about the queen as a role model than the king's feelings. To prevent a general epidemic of uppityness, they issued a fierce bulletin to all women, ordering them to treat their men as superiors from then on, whether they were or not.

And what of Vashti, the cool and gutsy queen who just said "No!" 2,300 years before Nancy Reagan thought of it? She was banished; most likely to her quarters or the main harem annex, not from the Earth. That's how Esther, her replacement, came to take center stage.

Prenuptials could be murder in old Mesopotamia. Just because her sister, **Taram**, was a priestess—exempting her from those tiresome childbearing chores—**Iltani** was on the permanent starting lineup for motherhood. The sisters married a Mr. Shamash in tandem. Instead of wedding cake, however, second-string Iltani got the dirty duty: baking bread for the household, carrying her sister's chair to the temple, even washing her sister's feet. But what really got her goat was the fine print of that dratted marriage contract: "When Taram's happy, Iltani better be happy, too." It was enough to make a surrogate mommy see red—except that blowing her top was taboo unless Taram was in a foul mood. Whether the sisters clashed or meshed is lost to history; but as a scary example of overenthusiastic legislation, shouldn't Iltani's 3,800-year-old case file be made required reading for today's lawmakers?

ESTHER

About 460 B.C., in a worldwide star search for a virgin with cover-girl looks for King Artaxerxes of Persia, Esther's name (which means "star") came up. Was this fate? No, Hollywood: Her real name was Myrtle. Myrt lived with her uncle Morty in Susa; both were part of the Jewish population who remained in Persia after the exile. The star-makers spent months lubing Esther with myrrh and other oils, the standard purification ritual, while Mort advised: "Smile, and for God's sake don't tell him you're Jewish."

At last Esther auditioned for the king, who liked what he saw, and, bingo, she was in . . . eventually (the Bible says she didn't get the ring for seven years). Despite new family ties, Morty got into a beef with the king's right-hand man, Haman, who decided to get rid of this upstart and his tribe as well. Using the king's seal, Haman issued a bogus order to destroy all Jews on a certain date. A panicky Morty leaned on Esther to lobby her man; she waffled until he said, "Star or not, you won't escape just because you're in the fancy house, Myrtle."

Meanwhile, Haman moved ahead with his personal holocaust, item one being Morty, and put up a giant gallows. That night, however, the king had insomnia and took to reading a ledger of court records as a cure. Running across an earlier good deed of Morty's, the king asked, "What'd we give the old boy for his loyalty?" and was told "Nothing." As usual, Haman was hanging around the palace, so the king said: "What do I give a guy I really want to honor?"

Smirking, Haman rattled off, "Oh, some nice duds, a crown, a triumph . . ."

"Do it," the king said, ordering him to lay the goods on Morty, which put Haman in a really foul mood.

Meanwhile, Esther had been busy, worrying herself sick over the fate of the Jews and arranging an intimate little dinner for Haman and the king. They showed up, and the king, feeling mellow, offered to grant her any wish. Esther screwed up her courage and said, "If I've found favor with you, then please spare my life and

Esther putting the finger on the fiendish Haman.

that of my people—for we're about to catch it big time from this fiend," pointing to Haman. Her disclosure ("You're Jewish?") blew the king's mind, and he stalked off into the garden. Haman used the opportunity to beg Esther for his life, throwing himself on the queen's couch to do so. The king returned and was even more annoyed, especially as Haman appeared to be jumping Esther's bones. A gallows being conveniently although inexplicably at hand, Haman was made its first customer.

Later that day, Uncle Morty was promoted to the king's right-hand spot. Amid the rejoicing, Esther reminded Artaxerxes that he hadn't eighty-sixed the fake "slaughter the Jews" decree. "Can't do that," he said. "But I can make it legal for Jews to fight for their lives." Which he did.

When the preemptive strike dust had settled, 75,000 Jewish enemies had died. Esther got Haman's property, and ordered up death for 500 of his allies in the palace. Thrifty as well as vengeful, she decided on hanging for Haman's ten sons ("Why let a perfectly good gallows go to waste?").

ROXANE & BARSINE

❀ ❀ ❀ ❀ ❀

Martha Stewart, eat your heart out—the most brilliant mass wedding in history happened 2,300 years ago. In the clear desert air of Susa, Alexander the Great and eighty of his Macedonian not-so-greats contracted marriage with an equal number of Persian beauties. His aim? To create an instant population mix, the better to attain world domination. Alex's own bride was a royal retread: Barsine-Stateira, the wife of Darius, the last Persian king, murdered shortly after Al beat the pants off him.

The wedding was the height of extravagance. Alexander (he would have made a fabulous caterer) immersed himself in every detail—with just a wee bit of help on fabrics from a cute Persian eunuch or two. In front of the palace, in a Superdome-sized, jewel-plastered pavilion, the ceremonies took place amid one hundred silvered couches and Persian carpets like you wouldn't believe. Five days of festivities alternated with five nights of newlywed bliss on silver beds courtesy of Alex (not-too-subtle hints of "Procreate, please!"). New heights may also have been reached by the Great One's bride. Half-sister as well as widow of six-foot-six-inch King Darius, she probably towered over Alex.

The one person who certainly did not attend this gala affair was Roxane, Alexander's own first wife. Bigamy wasn't the issue—power and maybe jealousy were. Emotionally and sexually speaking, Alex favored men; the first and only female he really fell for was Roxane, the arrogantly gorgeous daughter of an Afghani chieftain. On one of his conquer-all marches from here to there, Roxane danced for him, he proposed, and they had a month or two in the sack before he was off again. In their four-year marriage, Roxane had a stillborn baby and a son, so they slept together at least twice—unless you prefer to believe that a god impregnated her, which is what Alexander's mother often told him about his birth.

Roxane, stuck in Babylon, soon copped to the fact that Alex preferred conquering, drinking, naming cities after himself, his horse, and his male friend Hephastion to her. So she was even more bent out of shape when he made plans to marry the king of Persia's widow Barsine in the spectacle of the century. She shouldn't have worried about the new wife; Alex and Hephastion were still an item. Suddenly, however, Hephastion died in circumstances mysterious to almost everyone except perhaps Roxane. Within months, Alex himself fell ill and died. Chaos reigned. Roxane, now pregnant, instantly fired off a letter in Alex's name, asking Barsine to come to Babylon. Before you could say "bridal registry," Roxane had Barsine and her sister liquidated and tossed into a well. Killer style, that's what Roxane had—but not longevity. Post-Alex, she and her son were dispatched thirteen years later by the same general who murdered Alex's mom, Olympias.

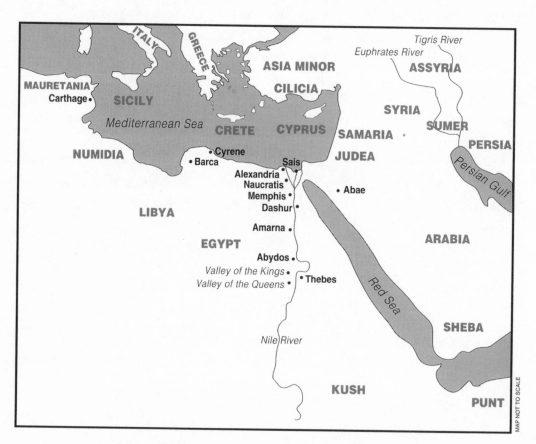

EGYPT & NORTH AFRICA

PHARAOHS, PHYSICIANS, FAT CATS & FILLY-FANCIERS

MERIT PTAH & COLLEAGUES

◆◆◆◆◆

The ancient Greeks were very impressed with Egyptian medicine, although they did think they went a little overboard on hygiene. (Can you believe it, these people wash their hands and plates after every meal! And that full-body hair removal—*really!*) A very anal bunch, Egyptians purged themselves monthly. Proctology got its real start here; doctors devoted entire books to lower gastrointestinal happiness.

"My daughter, the doctor" was a claim few parents in ancient Egypt could make. Yet women did become physicians, as these formidable females prove, the only mystery being the lack of detail that has survived about their careers.

Merit Ptah wins the "earliest female physician" sweepstakes. More than 4,700 years ago, she practiced medicine while the pharaohs began to build pyramids in earnest. Her son, a high priest, must have been proud of her. On her tomb in the Valley of the Kings, he put Merit's picture, taking care to label it "the chief physician."

Even after the regrettable asp incident, Cleopatra remained a popular female name in Egypt. In the second century A.D., another Cleo reaped fame for her medical writings on gynecology. Midwives and doctors, male and female, were to consult (and sometimes plagiarize) her material for another twelve centuries.

Then there was overachiever Peseshet, who gets the Order of the Golden Beeper for becoming not just a sawbones but a chief of women physicians. Although the correct reading of any hieroglyph can be an intellectual crapshoot, it's likely that her title indicates an administrator who oversees other (also female) doctors—a clue implying that women doctors were more than an isolated oddity here and there.

Egyptian women had to double as scribes and scholars just to study medicine, which in ancient times was an eclectic mix of efficacious herbs and treatments, a few timid surgical procedures, therapy via dream incubation, and plain old magic. Sometimes women apprenticed themselves to doctors to learn; they also, studied (and apparently taught) obstetrics and other specialties at medical facilities, such as the school in Sais, Egypt, that flourished around the sixth century B.C. Obstetrics was probably one of the more rewarding specialties. Given the Egyptian mania for keeping corpses intact to guarantee a great afterlife, it's a safe bet that female doctors in training didn't get to practice on any med school bodies.

When you ran the Egyptian version of a primp'n'perm thousands of years ago, as **Henut** did, you didn't worry about taking too much off the top. Women and men alike favored bald pates, shaved daily and topped with elaborate wigs to cut the heat and glare. Even on women who liked real tresses, Henut interwove false hairpieces. Her job description translates as "painter of her mouth," meaning she also acted as cosmetician to the queen. Besides painting the royal eyes with green malachite and black kohl, and her lips with red ochre and fat, Henut kept the queen sleek all over with a razor or that old favorite, a depilatory made of bat's blood. The artistry of Henut and other coiffure gurus, often depicted on the tomb reliefs of various queens, proves that women have believed they were worth it for more than 4,000 years.

MERYET-NEITH

Archaeologists call it "satellite burial," which sounds sanitary and tasteful. The people at Forest Lawn might call it "pre-need burial services." Whatever you call it, early rulers of Egypt, Mesopotamia, and elsewhere had a nasty habit of taking everything with them when they went. We're not talking about mere furniture, favorite foods, and cookware, either—but live pets, vehicles with real horsepower, and perfectly healthy people.

Meryet-Neith, a queen of Egypt's First Dynasty, and probably the very first Egyptian female to rule solo while her son Den was young, wanted lots of company in her eternal life. To get it, she built two tombs—an everyday one at Sakkara (near Cairo) and a huge and splendid affair at Abydos, to the south on the Nile River.

Her husband, King Djer, set the tone. When he expired around 3045 B.C., he took along three hundred of his retainers. Meryet-Neith, on the other hand, had to get by with barely forty-one members of her entourage, who were dressed to kill—or, in this instance, be killed. Needless to say, such practices caused enthusiasm for working for the likes of Meryet-Neith and Djer to sink to an all-time low, until someone decided it would be just as pleasing to the gods to have small human images called *shabtis,* instead of the rather cumbersome people themselves, as servants and tombmates.

AHOTEP

Now we know where the term *old battle-ax*, so often and lovingly used to refer to mothers-in-law, came from: Queen Ahotep. Married to her brother, Ahotep gave birth to Ahmose and later ruled in tandem with him. Motherhood was okay, but Ahotep loved military action: Planning battles and crushing rebels were her meat and drink. Around 1600 B.C., the Egyptians were fighting the Hyksos invaders, northern tough guys who used horse-drawn chariots in battle. Not about to be left out of the loop, she and the rest of the royal family hastily imported horses and soon had their own war chariot divisions at Thebes, their capital.

There was one thing, however, that Queen Ahotep just couldn't abide: military slackers. She took special pride in going after them herself, administering a fearsome justice. An inscription about her says, "She has looked after Egypt's soldiers; she has brought back her fugitives and collected together her deserters; she has pacified Upper Egypt, and expelled her rebels." For her efforts, Ahotep was three times given the fabulous Order of the Golden Fly, an award for valor. Carefully tucked in her tomb, archaeologists found her trio of 24-carat trophies, along with a ceremonial battle-ax overlaid with gold, electrum, and inlays.

HETEPHERES

Pharaoh Cheops, famed for building the Great Pyramid at Giza near Cairo, was also an only son who dearly loved his mother. Her name was Hetepheres, and she favored slippers of gazelle skin and dozens of silver ankle bracelets with tiny dragonflies of malachite on them. At night, she slept in an sleekly elegant bed whose gold footboard was painted with blue and black flowers. She laid her head on a curved wooden headrest, the Egyptian version of the pillow. Her chairs, her manicure set, even her razors were fashioned of gold. Hetepheres had need of those razors—Egyptians, male and female, shaved their heads and bodies every day.

Because the Egyptian habit of royal incest had matrilineal origins, Cheops traced his lineage through his mom. The oldest daughter of a reigning king was always called "the Daughter of the God's Body," and through her blood the succession passed. The best way for a royal prince to lock in his claim to the throne, then, was to marry his sister. Sometimes the family tree got so twisted that women had to marry their own fathers—or grandfathers.

We don't know the grand events of Hetepheres' life, just the odd story of her troubles after death. Because of her rank, she should have ended up snugly ensconced in her own small pyramid, near that of her husband, Sneferu. Robbers entered her tomb shortly after her burial, however. Looking for the quick score, the easy-to-fence stuff, they pried open her sarcophagus, snatched the jewelry, and ran. Her mummy disappeared, and only the canopic jars with her internal organs, now reduced to a sludge in embalming fluid, remained behind.

Even if he hadn't been fond of his mother, Cheops would have been appalled. For the Egyptians, messing with mummies was the worst kind of sacrilege. They believed that the most important rule for afterlife success was: Keep that body intact as a home for the person's *ka* spirit and the birdlike *ba* spirit. Without her mummy, Hetepheres' *ba* spirit, normally able to commute between the tomb and the outside world, was homeless. This was oblivion—the real death.

Terrified of the pharaoh's reaction, his underlings reburied Hetepheres' mummyless sarcophagus with some of her own furniture and belongings at an unmarked spot near Cheops' pyramid tomb at Giza. Four thousand years later, a photographer stumbled over the secret entrance to her second tomb, giving us a close look at the exquisitely beautiful details of her daily life. I hope her *ka* and *ba* are still in the area, and enjoying the modern admiration.

KHENTKAWES

Pyramid power wasn't confined to men or, in later times, even to royals. Several Egyptian queens busied themselves with vertical preparation for the afterlife. In front of the three-pyramid group at Giza, for instance, sit three smaller pyramids, each of them fit for a queen. That would be the chief queen, of course, called "the Great Royal Wife." Only Great Royals (and not all of them) got this perk; if all the second-string wives of pharaohs had gotten pyramids of their own, the Egyptian desert would be wall-to-wall by now.

Khentkawes, who lived around 2500 B.C., carried things even further. A variously married royal of the Fourth Dynasty whose alliances with brothers, half-brothers, and the like are still being argued over, she whipped up a structure for her final nap that still stands near the Sphinx. You couldn't really call it a pyramid—or a mastaba tomb, either. Mastabas have sloping sides and flat tops; they look like someone planned a pyramid and called the whole thing off about one-third of the way up. Like the Sphinx, Khentkawe's monument is enigmatic, a huge tomb cut from rock and then surrounded by a limestone building; below it, a corridor descends to a warren of burial chambers and rooms. At one corner, there is a boat-pit—no boat, just the pit. (Boat-pit amenities were fashionable for centuries—Cheops had one whose boat has survived.)

Everything about Khentkawe's life is puzzling. She's said to be the mother of two kings, but no one agrees which ones. After Khentkawes' death, a pharaoh thought to be one of her sons added another piece to the puzzle. He built a small pyramid for her at Abu Sir, now empty but still covered with her name and titles.

A nice boy, he didn't want her to go through eternity in a mastaba, which just doesn't cut it, magically speaking: In death, pyramids were the only way to go.

The last mysterious chapter about Khentkawes comes from that entertaining but not always reliable Greek historian, Herodotus, who spent time in Egypt around 450 B.C. While there, he went into a chamber and saw several statues with their hands missing. According to one account, Khentkawes had a daughter who killed herself because her father raped her. In her agony and rage, Khentkawes cut off the hands of the servants who had allowed the king access to the girl, then erected this disquieting reminder as a warning to those who would misuse a woman's body.

NITOCRIS

The study of women in history sometimes resembles quantum physics. To believe in subatomic particles or a woman like Nitocris, you accept certain premises on faith, because there's not much tangible proof.

Indeed, Queen Nitocris does sound a bit like a charmed quark. She lived and reigned in Egypt in the sometimes-misty beginnings of the twenty-first century B.C. Her family tree is a question mark; her dad might have been Pepi Two, a long-lived pharaoh who began his reign as a boy of six. Ancient historians loved cliché superlatives, especially for females. They called Nitocris "braver than all the men of her time" and "the most beautiful of all women." They also said one thing that sounded real: They said she had fair skin and rosy cheeks.

Nitocris came to the throne unwillingly. She was married to her brother, who was murdered—why, we don't know—by a mob of his subjects. This motley group of Egyptians then forced her to step up to the plate. For at least seven years, wearing "the Sledge and the Bee," the traditional crowns of Upper and Lower Egypt, Nitocris ran the country, but she remained curiously testy about her brother-husband's death. As therapy, she set about building a massive chamber underground, about the size of your average shopping mall. For the grand opening, she invited hundreds of Egyptians to the ribbon-cutting. Oddly enough, the guest list coincided with the cast of conspirators who had murdered her beloved.

So there they were, party in full swing, watching the acrobats and the dancing girls, knocking back cocktails and nibbling dormice and other ancient Egyptian hors d'oeuvres. In a move destined to gain her the nickname "party pooper of all time," Nitocris then locked her guests in the hall and opened a huge concealed conduit that let the waters of the Nile fill the room.

Unlike your true villains, Nitocris didn't really savor her wet-and-wild revenge or look forward to her punishment. Trying to top her own Guinness record for the most spectacular mass murder with one for the most difficult solo death, she committed suicide by flinging herself into a room packed with ashes. And, we presume, inhaling ever so deeply.

With their love of flawless skin on females, the Egyptians didn't think much of tattooing. Dancers such as **Isadora of Artemisia**, however, usually wore a tattoo of their patron god, lion-headed Bes, on their thigh. Egyptians adored dance. Performing around A.D. 200, Isadora and her troupe of castanet-clackers were part of a 3,000-year tradition that began as part of a religious ritual. By her day, dancers were de rigueur at all manner of private functions. A creative artist, Isadora was businesslike too, as her written agreement with an eager employer shows. For a six-day job, she and her troupe received thirty-six drachmas a day, plus all the barley and bread they could eat. To watch after the costumes and gold jewelry, the patron threw in security services. He even took care of transportation to and from the gig with a local "limo"—dual donkeys.

HATSHEPSUT

"Cross-dresser" was probably the nicest thing pharaoh-in-waiting Tutmose Three ever muttered about his aunt, the powerful and iron-willed Hatshepsut. His other remarks were unprintable. For twenty-one years, Hatshepsut kept him on hold, letting him play Prince Charles to her Queen Elizabeth.

First woman to become a full-on pharaoh, Hat had a career path with a bullet from the beginning. When her dad, Tut One, died around 1518 B.C., she married her half-brother, Tut Two. A normal strategy to bolster his right to govern—or so he thought. Hatshepsut had other goals. For fourteen years of "tandem" rule, she led, he followed. The only thing they collaborated on equally were daughters Nefrure and Hatti Junior.

About 1504, Tut Two died—to a sigh of relief from Hatshepsut, who sprang into action as regent to the young heir, Tut Three (her husband's only son by a harem girl). After a couple of years, with zero bloodshed or fuss, she left mere queenship behind and had herself formally proclaimed Female King of Egypt, taking on the five titles of a pharaoh, the male clothes, and the paraphernalia—even the false "beard of wisdom" each pharaoh wore. To clinch her silky smooth coup d'état, Hatshepsut gained the support of key officials, including her highest-ranking man, Senenmut, who tripled as steward, architect, and tutor to her daughter Nefrure.

To keep the pro-Tut faction cool, on paper it was a dual reign. Tut she married to Nefrure. Talk about a rock and a hard place: Poor Nefrure not only had the thankless task of marrying her restless half-brother, she had to snitch on his every move to her mother. As compensation, Hat gave her daughter the best hand-me-down gig she could think of: her own title of Divine Wife of Amun. The perks of the office made Nefrure owner of huge estates—small compensation for being in the cross-fire between Tut and the fiery female pharaoh.

With the help of Senenmut, Hatshepsut soon built a three-terraced temple, a propaganda piece she called "a garden for my father [the god] Amun." Set against the sheer coral cliffs at Deir el-Bahari, the temple later became famous for medical cures. She also put up two spectacular obelisks of red granite to glorify Amun (and Hat, of course) at Thebes.

A shrewd businesswoman, Hat mapped a daring itinerary for a trade expedition through the Suez Canal and south along the coast of Africa to the land of Punt. When her fleet successfully returned with a tangy cargo of cinnamon, myrrh trees, ebony, ivory, panther skins, ostrich eggs, and live baboons, the canny pharaoh sent more expeditions to the Sinai desert for turquoise and to other parts of Africa to collect wild animals for her new zoo, "the garden of Amun."

When Tut Three finally followed—or pushed—Hat out of the ring in 1483, he eventually hacked every mention of her name as Female King from the face of Egypt. Interestingly, he couldn't quite bring himself to obliterate Hatshepsut's name and image entirely, so statues and inscriptions of her name still exist in quantity—as queen, however, not as pharaoh.

Pharaoh dress code?
What dress code?

ETY

❖❖❖❖❖

She may have been pint-sized, pudgy, even partially deformed, but Queen Ety, nicknamed "the princess of Punt," stood tall in the world trade scene of the sixteenth century B.C. For Ety and Perehu, her long, lean Jack Sprat of a husband, life was good: they had a lock on the local frankincense and myrrh trade. Punt probably sat on the coast of East Africa, where Somalia is today. Its poor soil, rocky ravines, and gaspingly hot climate weren't good for much, but they suited the thorny myrrh bush and the scraggy frankincense trees just fine. Frankincense (meaning "true incense") and myrrh were the diamonds of the ancient world. Temples from Babylon to Greece to Judea used both by the shovelful, and potentates and princesses bathed in their oils. Myrrh had medicinal uses, too; wine-myrrh was a favorite burn remedy. Demand was high and supply was coyly limited to a few lands along the neighboring south Arabian and east African coasts, whose rulers created a Spice Curtain monopoly on the stuff for thousands of years.

To harvest incense, Queen Ety's workers gathered dried sap from the trees; others sorted the beads and grains for sale. Like diamond mining, everyone got a daily strip-search. Because frankincense and myrrh had holy associations, harvesting was done with care to avoid polluting actions.

One fine day in 1492 B.C., Queen Ety saw five sixty-foot ships near her shores, harps hanging from the masts as a signal of peace and friendship. The fleet belonged to female Pharaoh Hatshepsut. Although a long and difficult sail away from Punt, the Egyptians were famous for running through incense like you wouldn't believe. Ety probably rubbed her hands in glee and said, "Another live one!"

Little did she know at the time that her Egyptian dream client was planning to do some botanical cartel-breaking and grow her own. She soon caught on. Besides the vast quantities of myrrh and frankincense loaded into the ships' holds, the order included live plants. Thirty myrrh trees, carefully roped to contain their root balls, were taken on board.

Did Queen Ety maintain her virtual monopoly, or did King Hat succeed in her plans to grow Egyptian? According to one account, the trees, planted at the capital of Thebes, flourished. Although the trees have long since vanished, the holes carefully prepared for them have been found by archaeologists. Like Queen Ety's profitable enterprise in the unpromising soil of Punt, that's what you call making something out of nothing. Another something that came out of the trip to Punt was artistic immortality for Ety. An Egyptian artist accompanying the expedition made drawings of the fleet, the myrrh trees, the Puntites, and Queen Ety herself—all of which ended up as reliefs on the temple at Thebes.

TIYE

It got awfully crowded in the pharaoh's harem sometimes, but that was something Queen Tiye didn't have to worry about. As a teen, she married someone she actually cared for, and vice versa. Not only that, she and Amenhotep Three got hitched prior to his thirty-seven-year stint on the throne, before the real pressure was on.

Tiye had no royal blood coursing through her veins; her parents came from the Delta area of Egypt, where her dad was a military bigwig. (Theories abound that Tiye and her kin were Syrians, or blue-eyed Aryans, or Hittites, or from the lost tribe of Israel, or black Nubians from Kush, a country located in today's Egypt and the Sudan. Sorry, conspiracy fans—the much-scrutinized mummies of Tiye's folks indicate that they're Egyptians; in keeping with their Bobbsey-twin names of Yuya and Tuya, they both had long, reddish-gold hair.)

A woman of abundant vitality and good sense, Tiye also had a flair for political astuteness that improved with age. Unlike some other pharaohs I could name, her appreciative husband liked to put his affection in tangible form while his wife was still above ground. Once he created a mile-long lake in the desert for Tiye; the couple used to go for sundowner cruises in the royal barge, called *The Aten Gleams*. A nice way to get away from the kids—four daughters and two sons. Only one boy survived; in pharaoh fashion, Amenhotep set about dutifully procreating with his daughters as soon as they were old enough.

Another of Amenhotep's love gestures to Tiye was even more meaningful, especially if you were an ancient Egyptian: On many reliefs and sculptures, he ordered his-and-her portraits that were equal in size. This may not seem like a major breakthrough to you and me, but it was a radical departure from the norm of the time. The rule was: pharaohs big; women, kids, and inferiors (dirty foreigners, et cetera) small—sometimes antlike.

As a widow, Tiye had to weather part of the turbulent reign of her son Akhenaten, who wanted to put Egypt on a one-god system; he set about doing it overnight, moving the capital city and ignoring affairs of state. Not only did this throw Egypt into political turmoil, but Tiye had to put up with the godlike ambition of her own niece and daughter-in-law, Nefertiti. Just as well Tiye didn't survive to see the stunted last act of her Eighteenth Dynasty—her short-lived and golden stepson Tutankhamen.

NEFERTITI

It's not a stretch to call Queen Nefertiti the Jackie Kennedy of her day. An international household name, she didn't just set fashion—she *was* fashion. Cameras would have loved her telegenic profile and the jazzy blue turban she made hers alone. Her imagery showed up everywhere: on wall reliefs, statues, busts, rings, and scarabs. A commoner like her aunt Tiye, Nefertiti followed in her footsteps, also marrying a man who became pharaoh. But a huge philosophical gap existed between Amenhotep Three and his son—and between Tiye and her glamorous niece.

Nefertiti, whose name means "the beautiful one has arrived," and the big-jawed, baggy-bellied man she married, were big-picture thinkers. Their political goal: to break away from the mummified weight of the past, to create an Egyptian Camelot where the arts, culture, and religious worship could take on new vitality and freedom. A pretty big menu, but this bold, brainy, and unusually demonstrative pair of leaders relished the challenge. Encouraged by Nefertiti, who took an active part in the top-to-bottom change, her husband tossed out the old gods and rang in a semi-new one: Aten, the sun-god. Now calling himself Akhenaten, the pharaoh and Nefertiti were the only ones allowed to serve the god; this meant pink slips all around for the huge priestly population. To further tee everyone off, the royal family and court left the capital of Thebes and built a fancy new garden city (now the el-Amarna archaeological site) dedicated to Aten.

Why is it that Camelots always seem to have more than their share of tragedy? Three of their six daughters died young, political pressures made life difficult, and Akhenaten began to backpedal in his beliefs. (That's one theory of what came between this couple; the clues are contradictory, so it's a game anyone can play.) In the twelfth year of her husband's reign, Nefertiti's name simply vanishes, replaced by a daughter as Great Royal Wife. Now this was a woman who got more public exposure than Jackie O. herself. Could she have remained in Amarna as it slowly decayed? Did she outlive her husband—or try for the throne? The mysteries surrounding her remain unsolved—and now the beautiful one has gone.

"My garland of daughters," Queen Nefertiti called **Meritaten** and her younger sisters, six happy little girls who lived around 1330 B.C. in Thebes. Princesses grew up fast in Egypt; when things got sticky between Meritaten's formerly loving parents, Nefertiti was either ousted or died, and Meritaten had to marry her own father, Akhenaten. She took the title of Great Royal Wife, and had a baby daughter, named Meritaten Junior. Although evidently virile, her father had mysterious afflictions which no one has figured out, including a bizarrely elongated jaw and hips that a Renoir nude would be proud to own. As he went downhill, he looked to his half-brother Smenkhare to succeed him, and Meritaten, as Great Royal Wife, to make him more eligible to rule. She probably didn't live to see Smenkhare as pharaoh. A short life, but perhaps a happy one: Unlike the rigidly formal life led by Egyptian royals to that point, Meritaten and her sisters were part of their parent's quest for individualism. At Amarna, religious changes opened the door for other kinds of change. Artists were free to portray people as they really were—or weren't. For centuries, Amarna impressionism infused art with new vitality; one treasure left to us is a portrait head of a woman both smart and sensual, now thought to be Meritaten.

ANKHESENAMUN

Consanguineous marriage, a term that means "keep the royal blood in the family at all costs," led to some pretty weird carnal arrangements. Ankhesenamun, who couldn't have seen more than twenty-two birthdays in her life, may take the cake for Egypt's strangest string of sex partners.

The third daughter of Nefertiti and Ankhenaten, she grew up in a rollicking family group. As a child, she and her sisters ran about naked, just like other children, her hair pulled to the side in a topknot. At the brand-new garden city of Amarna, life was sunny in their shiny new palace. Like her sisters, she had to mature pronto. When her older sister Meritaten died, it was Ankhesenamun's turn to do her dynastic duty. In rapid-fire succession, she had to marry (and bury) three brothers: her pharaoh father, her uncle Smenkhare, and finally Tutankhamen, who was all of nine years old. The too-knowing teen no doubt felt more like his sister—which she also was.

Their marriage lasted ten years. Just before Tut's death in his teens, they had two babies, neither of which survived. By now, Ankhesenamun was pretty fed up with the notion of consanguinity. She also feared there was worse in store. For decades, a shadowy figure behind the throne had run things more and more. He was Ankhesenamun's own grandfather, Ay, a powerful commoner and the father of Nefertiti.

As the priests began Tut's mummification and burial, the young widow knew she had just seventy days to carry out her plans. She sent an urgent message to Suppliliumas, the Hittite king to the north of Egypt, which said: "My husband's died, and not one son do I have. I've heard you have many—will you send one to be my husband? I will never accept marrying one of my servants." The Hittite king, blown away yet suspicious, made inquiries about the reliability of the offer. Meanwhile, the clock was ticking on Tut's embalming.Exasperated, Ankhesenamun shot off another note, saying, "This isn't a mass mailing, Suppi—I haven't written anyone else—just you. Send me a spare son pronto, and I'll make him my husband and king of Egypt!" Convinced at last, the king sent his son Zannaza, but the young prince was intercepted and killed before his arrival, confirming her fears about the situation. The

clock ran out; she was married to a sixty year old whom she considered both despicable and beneath her, grandfather or not. At Tut's funeral, Ankhesenamun, already wed to the old man, placed a wreath of flowers on her boy lover's forehead, the last documented act of a courageous girl who'd had to live too much, too soon.

MAKEDA

◆◆◆◆◆

Three thousand years before oil cartels, Queen Makeda, ruler of sweet-smelling Sheba (probably Yemen in Arabia plus the nearby portion of Ethiopia), had built herself a nice spice near-monopoly. Sheba didn't have much else, but its land was so dense with balsam, myrrh, cassia, and other fragrant herbs that the intoxicating scent of the blooms could be detected by voyagers offshore.

Myrrh, balm, and other spices had many virtues: low bulk, high price, long shelf life, and in heavy demand for medicine, flavoring, meat preservation, religious use, and room deodorizers. A canny trader, Makeda knew that expansion of her trade networks would make the Sheba bottom line look really good. With that in mind, she planned a sales trip to a client who used more incense than almost anyone—King Solomon, 2,000 miles north as the camel plods, in Jerusalem.

In their first "perfume summit" meeting, the queen took stock of Solomon, seeing a man with charm and brains. Makeda had a thing for philosophy as well as more practical matters; she'd brought some tough questions for the king. On the negative side, she saw a guy with major financial worries. That palace with its forest of Lebanon tree pillars and cool throne room looked great, but it was costing him an arm and a leg. The man supported nearly a thousand wives and concubines, all eating three squares a day, and no steam-table menus, either.

After Makeda laid her caravan loads of jewels, gold, and spice samples on him, they had a few drinks and she got the inside story: King Solomon was running a heavy deficit. For income, he leaned on his copper and iron mines and a few retail ventures in chariots and horses, but it was far from enough. He'd already taxed the almighty out of his citizens, and even put some free Jews to work at forced labor. Makeda saw his only quick-fix way to squeeze more revenue was to hike tolls and customs fees—a move that would bite into her margin in a mean way.

Makeda had some serious lobbying to do. Besides, she kinda had the hots for Solomon, and he for her. Six months later, she left for home with the things she wanted—and a few she hadn't counted on: her memories of a heavy romance, including a "souvenir" in the form of a baby to be; 120 talents in gold (roughly $5 million in today's terms); new diplomatic ties; and an amazingly good mutual trade agreement.

Back in Sheba, she gave birth to a son named Menelik, and let Solomon know. Bad move: When he learned about the boy, he went all bossy, decreeing that only the male heirs of their child should rule *her* land. Wouldn't you know it, for most of the centuries since Solomon, the rulers of Ethiopia through Emperor Haile Selassie have been doing just that?

SHEPENWHEPET

The Egyptians may not have had rock and roll, but some of the names and titles they handed out could easily appear on the cover of *Rolling Stone* magazine. Shepenwhepet, for instance. Or how about the Divine Adoratrice? That one's got a real Whitney Houston ring.

As it happened, the mellifluous-sounding Shepenwhepet Two was both a Divine Adoratrice and a woman of real staying power. During her lifetime in the seventh century B.C., the Assyrians (the spiritual ancestors of Nazi Germany's storm troopers) were on the prowl. Led by a couple of Assyria's most vicious kings, they easily squashed Egypt's neighbors and ripped into the land of the pharaohs with both booted feet.

As Divine Adoratrice, Shepenwhepet Two controlled the huge priesthood of Amun, a bureaucratic maze of temples, priests, lands, properties, and revenues. Previously, the equally prestigious office of God's Wife or Divine Wife had been held by a succession of royal princesses, who kept up the god's cult on behalf of the king. Now the duties and authority of the Chief Priestess of Amun and God's Wife were rolled into one. Besides raw power, the Divine Adoratrice had other perks: short hours, no lifting, got to be called "Your Majesty," and no kids or husbands to look after or answer to.

The prestige of the office was such that amid all the carnage between Assyrians and Egyptians, Shepenwhepet Two tranquilly remained in office. The pharaoh's wife and family might be carried off to Assyria, the pharaoh himself stabbed five times with a javelin, the Egyptian cities of Thebes and Memphis burned down, the male population slapped in chains, but nobody messed with the Divine Adoratrice.

There was a downside, of course: those nagging vows of chastity. Since children were out of the picture, Shepenwhepet Two had to "adopt" a daughter to succeed her, as all Divine Adoratrices did. In turn, her new daughter Nitocris built her a mortuary chapel, complete with a guarantee that offerings were to be made for Shepenwhepet, quote, "throughout eternity."

The favorite first wife and Chief Queen of Ramses Two, **Nefertari** wasn't the whole enchilada by any means—her equal opportunity husband married Hittites, Syrians, Babylonians, and a batch of his own daughters. But even in a crowd, gorgeous and well-loved Nefertari stood out. If you were married to a pharaoh who wanted to show he cared, he didn't bring home jewelry or appliances. He laid out serious cash to make sure your afterlife was splendid. In the Valley of the Queens, Ramses Two built Nefertari a tomb to die for—or in. Every square inch glows with color and art, from the star-studded ceiling to the frescos of Nefertari making offerings and playing *senet*, the Egyptian version of chess. Senet, with its dual meanings of "passing" and "to endure," must have been the game of choice for the tomb—a comforting thought for a beautiful queen and the grieving husband she left behind in 1255 B.C.

PHERETIMA

◆◆◆◆◆

Until modern times, people sort of expected death to be early and/or painful. For instance, Heraclitus, a famous sixth-century B.C. philosopher, tried to cure his dropsy by burying himself neck-deep in dung, whereupon local dogs found him irresistible and ate him. It's hard to top such a spectacular signout, but the grisly finale of Pheretima, a contemporary of his, may come close.

She was First Lady of Cyrene, a fertile and scenic stretch along the North African coast, colonized a hundred years earlier by the islanders of Thera on a nudge from the prophetess at the oracle of Delphi: "Great weather, you'll love it." On the minus side, Pheretima was married to a no-luck king named Battus. Lameness ran in his family, literally and every other way. Even though they lived in a piece of paradise, under his inept management things kept going wrong. When he died, Queen Pheretima and her son Arcesilaus tried to reverse his actions, which led to civil war. The son fled one way, and Pheretima ran up to the island of Cyprus, where she nicely asked the king for an army to recapture her throne. He rudely responded with a set of wool-making implements in gold—his idea of a joke about "women's work." Meantime, Sonny had rustled up an army elsewhere; before heading back to the capital city of Cyrene, however, he checked in at the Delphic oracle, where he got a psychic update (did these people run a tab, or what?). He ignored the oracle, who told him not to proceed, and was murdered right on schedule when he went into Cyrene's city, Barca.

Although she had things back to normal, Pheretima was forced to drop everything and flee again. This time she headed for Egypt and talked its leader into helping her siege Barca; she sent a message to the citizens: Cut loose the culprit who killed my son, or this embargo's gonna get dirty. "We all killed him," responded those darned Barcans. On went the siege for nine dreary months. Finally the Persians, who wanted peace in Cyrene so they could do some mining business, acted as go-betweens and delivered the guilty parties to Pheretima. She could have been magnanimous, but *no . . .* By now in a flaming snit, she decided to redecorate, adorning the city walls with stakes that held the impaled heads of the murderers and the breasts of their wives. For an encore, she let the Persians pillage and make slaves of the Barcans.

After the Barca bloodbath, Pheretima made an unpublicized exit to Egypt. But she just wasn't fated to relax, enjoy retirement, and go over old memories. Instead, she came down with an ailment so ghastly the Greeks didn't even have a name for it (neither do we). Her body began to seethe with worms, which consumed her while she was still alive, right down to the last bite.

ARSINOE

"When in doubt, snuff 'em out" worked for Arsinoe Two, most uppity and political of the murderous Macedonians and triple winner in the advantageous marital sweepstakes. Married at sixteen to sixty-something Lysimachus, king of Thrace, she gave him three sons and swept this sugar daddy off his feet. In turn, he gave her several nice trinkets belonging to an ex-wife, including a huge chunk of real estate around the Black Sea. Arsinoe didn't have to fake it long. Soon after chiding her for doing in her stepson, Lysimachus got killed in battle, and Arsinoe left for the bright lights of Ephesus. Her half-brother now asked if she wanted to become queen of Macedon by hitching up with him; turned out what he really yearned to do was to put his hands on Arsinoe's sons. In no time, two were dead, one fled. Needless to say, that marriage had a short half-life.

Third time's a charm, however: Arsinoe latched onto her younger brother, Ptolemy Two, pharaoh of Egypt. At the time, he was a bit tied up, what with mistresses and a wife named Arsinoe One, but our Two got her trashed and banished before you could say prenuptial agreement. Always the careful homemaker, Arsinoe made things tidy by accusing all potential rivals of treason and having them swept out as well.

The sibling lovebirds settled in for a long co-reign. Despite his quirks—swarms of mistresses, bad taste in furniture—Ptolemy Two was a doer. He built the lighthouse at Pharos so Alexandria would have its own wonder of the world, he collected animals for the zoo, and he got the Museum of Alexandria and its library rolling. Arsinoe was more than a match for him. Strong-willed, ambitious, a real beauty with a gift for getting her own way, she became a key figure in court politics. She's generally credited with spearheading Egypt's growth into a marine power. Among her brainier moves was to not have any children with Ptolemy ("What the heck, they just grow up and kill you anyway.")

Naturally, she got her own coinage. Arsinoe also thought goddess status might be a thrill, so she encouraged the growth of Arsinoe worship. Who knows what heights she might have reached had she not died at age forty-five? Despite his female sidelines, Ptolemy was genuinely distraught. In a flash, he had Arsinoe made into a major-league goddess, renamed cities for her, and planned a high-tech temple with a vast statue of her suspended in midair by monster lodestones (natural magnets). Sadly, both architect and pharaoh died before it was finished, so Arsinoe's high-flying memorial remained metaphorical.

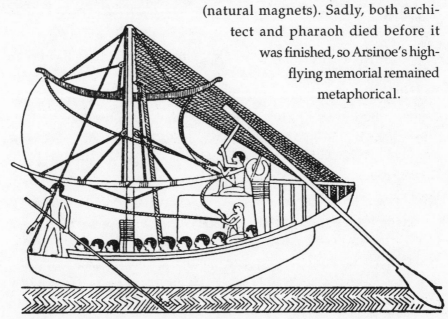

BILISTICHE

For a Macedonian miss who had a thing for fillies and phony pharaohs, Bilistiche didn't make out too badly. Born around 280 B.C., she lived during the exciting times when the not-so-great successors to Alexander the Great busied themselves with mutual murder, constantly redivvying the pie of Alex's fragile empire.

Bilistiche gravitated to Egypt, where she hooked onto Ptolemy Two, who ruled as monarch and pharaoh. Her boyfriend was a dirty old man—and a busy one, too. Married to his sister Arsinoe Two (which accounts for his nickname, "sister lover"), he collected so many girlfriends he must have needed an appointments secretary just for his romances.

Naturally, he told Bilistiche, "You're the one, Bili babe—the rest are just window dressing." In her case, he may have meant it. She was a front-runner in more ways than one. A racehorse freak, Bilistiche heard about the new Olympic Games event for chariot racing with a pair of colts and got antsy to enter. A little cajoling of her newly widowed sweet Ptolemy, and she got what she needed. She won the event in the One Hundred Twenty-Ninth Olympiad. A naughty poem of that era makes it clear that Bilistiche was a good rider; still, she may not have driven the pair herself. For the horse events, the owners often hired charioteers or riders.

Arsinoe's death gave Ptolemy more free time to pamper his Macedonian mistress, laying numerous religious honors on her which raised male hackles around the Med. At age thirty or so, Bilistiche was made *canephore* priestess, a job normally requiring a virgin with a good rep who could do a little light lifting. Unruffled by having almost none of these qualifications, Bilistiche blithely led a huge annual religious procession through the streets of Alexandria, carrying a canephore, or basket of gold offerings, on her head.

An enthusiastic builder, Ptolemy then erected a temple to a made-up deity called Aphrodite Bilistiche in honor of his mistress. This threw locals into fits. A poet named Sotades wrote a grotesque poem about it and, for good measure, mentioned the pharaoh's dead sister-wife Arsinoe. Making a mockery of the sexual extravagances of His Pharaohship wasn't such a good idea; the poet ended up six fathoms deep in a chest made of lead.

Still-buoyant Bilistiche continued her winning streak into old age. What with the generous way her royal honey paid for her time and the racehorses she owned and ran, her golden years were just that. A document from 239 B.C. shows that Bilistiche made her money work even harder in her final career of her life: money-lender. Knowing her keen eye for the odds, I don't think any of them were low-interest loans.

SOPHONISBA

Like their men, the women of Carthage, superpower on North Africa's coast, were fighters. They reveled in defiant acts, like the one Sophonisba made around 205 B.C.

When Hannibal, their ace general, first took his troops and elephants over the Alps to fight the Romans, things went his way. Time after time, he won decisive battles, but was never able to make Italy a wrap. After ten years of this, money was tight, tempers were short, and the situation in Italy and in Hannibal's home city of Carthage was last-ditch.

Daughter of a Big Man about Carthage named Hasdrubal, Sophonisba had beauty and wit to spare. To save her city, she willingly let herself be a pawn in the political stakes. First she married Syphax, a strong-man king of Numidia; with her sexual allure as prime motivator, she turned his alliance from the Romans to her people. The Romans being pretty crafty themselves, they then negotiated with another Numidian king, Masinissa, setting him to fight Syphax—and win.

When Sophonisba saw Masinissa stroll into her palace fully armed, she got the drift—time to dish up another serving of humble pie. Getting down on her knees, she said, "Check it out, Masinissa, one minute I'm queen of Numidia, and the next, I'm your slave. But hey—you're welcome to the merchandise—I'd rather die at your hands than fall into Roman ones."

Numidians being noted for hot qualities, Masinissa fell into instant lust. He married her while the Romans were still busy sacking Carthage. After a one-night honeymoon, Masinissa had to report back to the Roman military camp. He arrived with a few necessary items in tow—sackfuls of booty, his royal servants, and his new wife Sophonisba. Scipio, the head general for the Romans, took him to task. "Haven't you heard? It's against regulations to marry a captive." Masinissa sniveled all the way back to his tent, where he had his servant whip up a cup of poison and deliver a no-frills ultimatum to his new bride.

Some newlywed gift—a choice of suicide weapons

After hearing his "Sorry it didn't work out—here's your chance to stay out of Roman hands" message, Sophonisba was only too happy to grab the cup of Jonestown juice. As her parting shot, she said: "I willingly accept this wedding gift—but tell that noxious Numidian that I would've died better if I hadn't married at the point of death." Romans, Carthaginians, and Numidians alike praised her enormously for this. They admired the concept of noble suicide by young, firm, uppity women—so much easier to honor them dead than to deal with them alive.

THAIS OF ALEXANDRIA

Alexandrians were very good at inventing things, but inventions are like children: You put them out there, but you really don't know how they're going to end up. About 150 B.C., a local barber named Ctesibus was messing around, trying to counterbalance a shop mirror. In the process, he made a rude noise with compressed air, giving him the idea for an instrument to play music. He called it the *hydraulis* or "water organ." You sat at the thing, shaped like a round altar, and played the keys.

Thais, his wife, was quite taken with the device. Once Ctesibus had the kinks worked out, he taught Thais to play as well. Soon the sweet and happy sound of the water organ swept the Mediterranean. By Roman times, hydraulis musicians played at weddings, swearing-ins, theater intermissions, and other public events. I suppose it was inevitable that Nero, the "I did it my way" emperor and wannabe artiste, would take it up. Worse yet, the hydraulis became the instrument of choice to accompany the bloody gladiatorial contests. Sometimes backed up by a horn or two, the organist (usually female) ground through old favorites while gore-covered combatants ground through each other. Thais didn't have a clue what she set off; her achievement may have started the trend toward women hydraulis players, even in the most appalling of settings.

HELENA OF ALEXANDRIA

A mural painter, Helena lived and worked in Alexandria, Egypt, when the deeds and the image of Alexander the Great were still as sharp as crystal in everyone's mind. The city of her birth was practically brand-new, founded by Alex in 332 B.C.

Helena and Timon, her father and painting mentor, both followed Protogenes and the Asiatic school. That doesn't mean they did Chinese calligraphy; in ancient times, "Asia" signified Asia Minor, or what we would call Turkey plus parts of Syria and Iraq.

No painter of pretty posies, she liked to portray battle scenes and other carnage on frescoes and canvas. Her masterpiece was a battle scene of Issus, a narrow coastal plain in Asia Minor, where Alexander the Great beat the socks off the Persians in 333 B.C. Centuries after her death, in Emperor Vespasian's reign, a fan purchased this bravura piece of Helena's and took it to Rome, where it hung in the Forum of Peace (an odd place to hang a scene of exquisite violence, but painters—especially long-dead ones—can't be too choosy). That work no longer exists. But we know what Helena's style might have been like. Her painting is said to have inspired the most famous mosaic in the world: a riveting composition of Alexander the Great on horseback, sword in hand, his far-gazing eyes already on future conquests. That mosaic came to light in our century, on the floor of the villa of the Faun in Pompeii.

BERENICE

One gentle and virtuous exception to the mayhem-prone Macedonian rulers of Egypt was Berenice Two, who lived just down the road from Alexandria in Cyrene, a wealthy colony of rich wheat fields and vineyards established by the Greeks in the sixth century. Her dad fussing from the sidelines, Berenice toyed with two kingly fiancés and finally married a third—the pleasingly plump pharaoh, thirtysomething Ptolemy Three. His first act was to suck Cyrene into Egypt's orbit (he called it "reuniting"); his second, to rename one of its cities after Berenice. The couple soon had a son, predictably porky and named Ptolemy Four.

Suddenly, a news flash from Syria: Seems that Berenice's brother-in-law had croaked—either bad fish or an ex-wife's handiwork. Off went Ptolemy to rescue his sister. Before he got there, the ex had poisoned her and their son as well. All that was left to do was whale the daylights out of the city of Antioch. Once in Syria, he wrote Berenice, saying: "While I'm in the area, I might as well ravage Babylon—retrieve those religious statues the Persians stole from us way back when. Be home soon, honey."

Berenice cared about her husband; in an unusual gesture, she cut off her long locks of honey gold and dedicated them to the temple goddess for his safe return. For five years, she ran Egypt, making a very competent head of state. When Ptolemy returned, religious goodies in hand, everyone was tickled. Berenice dragged him to the temple to show him her lucky hair, but the tresses had vanished. To console her, a famous astronomer in her court said her curls had been carried to the heavens, and pointed to a new star cluster which he named "Coma Berenices" or "Berenice's Hair." (It's still up there.)

Berenice became a widow in 221 B.C. and ruled with her son Ptolemy Four. But not for long. Within a year, the Macedonian cruel and drunken streak reasserted itself, and the appreciably fatter, tipsier, and meaner new pharaoh had his mom poisoned and, for an encore, scalded his little brother.

At first glance, the short life and career of **Makare** seems straightforward enough. An Egyptian princess, she and her niece married a high priest of Amun in one of those Egyptian ménage à trois situations. Makare may have had to split a husband, but she got some great titles out of the deal: "Divine Wife of the god Amun," "Divine Votaress," and "Hand of the God," which referred to the way the god Amun had brought his children into the world—via masturbation. Despite being married, Makare as Divine Votaress remained a virgin—or was supposed to. Three thousand years later, however, an x-ray of her mummy revealed that just before she died she appeared to have given birth. That was excitement enough, but then came another find: The small, mummified bundle tucked in her coffin, which archaeologists had assumed was her infant, turned out to be a female baboon! Some theorize the primate had religious significance; others claim it must have been a pet. Mysterious Makare and her mystifying mummymate may not have counted on this sort of scientific immortality, but they've got it.

HERAIS

◆◆◆◆◆

Logical minds of our era might find unconditional belief in the ancient oracles hard to swallow. Now it's quite possible that some oracles also used nonpsychic sources (secret agents, passenger-pigeon air mail) to make predictions. Nevertheless, some of their spectacular and weird bull's-eyes make subterfuge seem unlikely.

Take the case of Herais, for example, which happened around 148 B.C. An oracle of Apollo at Cilicia (part of Turkey) told an ambitious young sprout named Alexander Balas to "beware of the place that bore the two-formed one." Balas tucked away this enigmatic fortune cookie and went about his business of warfare, eventually finding himself in Arabia, in a Greek-founded city called Abae.

Abae spelled home to a gal named Herais, who'd recently been given by her father in marriage to Samiades, a traveling salesman of some sort. After a year of wedded bliss, Sam went on a year-long business trip. In his absence, Herais got sicker than a dog. A large and painful tumor began to grow in her abdomen. Doctors did what they could for her fever and pain, to little effect. After a week, the darn thing burst, and out popped a complete three-piece set of male genitals. Wouldn't you know it, the doctors were playing golf, so only Herais' mom and a couple of female servants caught the transformation. Dumbfounded, they kept it all in the family. Upon recovering, Herais put on regular women's clothing and kept on acting like a housewife.

Samiades finally showed up, now eager for a little intimate pillow talk. Everybody put him off: Herais, the servants, her mom, and even her dad, who was just too embarrassed to tell Sam he was bedding down with a guy now. Sam got so hot he took the whole family to court, suing Herais' father to return his wife to him. The jury found for the husband, saying it was her wifely duty to get in the sack with him. Herais had no option but to let it all hang out in court, protesting that the law shouldn't require her to cohabit with a man now that she was a him.

Once everyone got over the shock, Herais threw on some manly duds, changed her name to Diophantus, and joined the cavalry unit of Alexander Balas so she could do guy stuff, like pillage and fight. Balas then had a small setback, retreating with his troops to Abae, where he was assassinated by two of his oldest friends—and, shazam! a distant oracle scores again.

Good old Sam, meanwhile, found that he still loved Herais. Since the formerly female Herais was now out of the picture, the heartbroken husband in limbo wrote out a will, made the new and improved Diophantus his heir, and killed himself.

CLEOPATRA SEVEN

Famed as a glamorous party animal and a grand schemer, Cleopatra Seven was also an intellectual, a linguist, and a pretty darn good mother. Born in 69 B.C. to a flabby Ptolemy nicknamed "The Flute Player," this Cleo hadn't lost it through inbreeding. Clever and motivated, she loved to read, deriving a sensuous pleasure from literature and soaking up languages like a sponge. By the time she and brother Ptolemy Thirteen began to reign, she spoke Greek, Hebrew, Arabic, Persian, and Egyptian—the only queen in three hundred years to learn the local tongue.

Julius Caesar came to Egypt (at that time free but greedily coveted by Romans and others) looking for support and any loose cash, and found a polyglot sexpot instead. The attraction put Cleo in the driver's seat. Within a year, she gave birth to Julius' son, Caesarion, and Ptolemy Thirteen was conveniently dead. Cleopatra then married her eleven-year-old brother, young Ptolemy Fourteen. Year 45 B.C. was a high-water mark: Cleo lived openly as Caesar's mistress in Rome, and even got her statue in the temple of Venus. Romans didn't like it one bit, however, and soon planned an Ides of March surprise assassination party for dictator Caesar.

Cleopatra scuttled back to Egypt, thinking hard all the way. Her first act was to kill brother Ptolemy; her second, to put Julius' three-year-old son on the throne. Two years later, Mark Antony, ruler of the east part of the Roman Empire, shows up. Chemistry (with a little mutual calculation) strikes again. Hard-drinking, bullishly handsome, and bad with details, Antony developed his own stud shuttle service, commuting between wife Fulvia in Rome and Cleo in Egypt. In 40 B.C., while Cleo was busy having his twins, he was busy marrying a third wife, Octavia. Cleo chose to ignore this, and stayed faithful to him as she was to Julius. Five years later, she and Mark had another son. To tutor this flock of kids, Cleopatra hired Philostratus and Nicolaus, philosopher and historian heavyweights, who joined other thinkers, poets, and scientists as part of her court. While continuing to reign as queen of Egypt with her son Caesarion, she studied philosophy, traveled and partied with Mark, developed a goiter (could it be those lavish dinners and drinks?), and got in a little reading (one of Mark's gifts to her was the huge Pergamum library).

Even killer queens make good moms

The high life on royal barges was grand, but Cleo never lost sight of her goal: to keep Egypt—looked on by Rome as a conveniently weak and filthy rich breadbasket—as independent as possible. So Mark and Cleo bet the farm and ended up losing both their fleets to Octavian. To add insult to injury, Octavian then grabbed Egypt as his personal estate rather than as a Roman province. It was high time to bring on that asp, Cleo thought. Before she died, however, she reacted as a mother, sending Caesarion to India to try to get him out of harm's way. Another mom thought about Cleo's other kids: Strangely enough, they found a haven with Octavia, Mark Antony's compassionate wife, who raised them with her own.

THE OTHER CLEOPATRAS

"Serpent of the Nile" Cleopatra, imprinted for centuries on our brains by everyone from Shakespeare to e. e. cummings, grabbed all the breathless press. She was actually Cleo number seven of a Macedonian dynasty. Between 200 B.C. and 50 B.C., there were more Cleopatras (numbered and unnumbered) than *Rocky* sequels. Unlike *Rocky,* however, the Cleos tended to get better—or at least leaner, meaner, and more ambitious.

The first Cleo, nicknamed "the Syrian," had boldness, brains, and bucks to spare. Daddy Antiochus laid a modest dowry on her—the countries of Syria, Samaria, Judea, and Phoenicia—which gave her a certain amount of clout around the palace in Memphis, Egypt. In his reign, her waffly young husband, Ptolemy Five, managed to lose most of these shiny new possessions. He and Cleo celebrated his nonexistent triumphs by putting up the Rosetta Stone, which later proved useful for deciphering hieroglyphics. On his death, she competently ruled for eight years, putting out the first Cleo currency and putting off her cranky pop, who now wanted back what was left of his dowry lands.

Cleo Three was the sister of "the Syrian"; she and Cleo Two, daughter of "the Syrian," really got fem rule cranking on the Egyptian throne, mostly by marrying every Ptolemy in sight and giving birth to a crop of successively more unpleasant and dissipated new ones. Cleos Two and Three both married Ptolemy Eight, a repulsive old soul nicknamed "Pot Belly," and agreed to rule as joint queens. In her own sequel, Cleo Three also ruled with her son Ptolemy Nine, called "Chick-Pea," finally running him off on a trumped-up mother-murder plot, and taking

Ptolemy Ten—her other son—to bed. It must have been king-sized; the inbred Ptolemy men ran to fat, but Ten could barely walk. Cleo Three died at age sixty, perhaps pushed (or sat on) by her son. The other Cleopatras in the series led equally active and ambitious lives; several, however, had the dubious distinction of being murdered by their sister Cleos.

After the spectacular life and suicide of megastar Cleopatra Seven, her namesake daughter was all but forgotten to history. The orphaned Eight, Cleopatra Selene (whose name means "moon") and twin brother Alex Helios ("sun") grew up in Rome. Serene Selene got married to Juba, becoming queen of Mauretania, a huge Roman district on the picturesque North African coast of present-day Morocco. They reigned for nearly fifty years, had two kids, and enjoyed Greek arts and culture—a strangely peaceful-sounding end game to the turbulent dynasty of the Cleopatras.

DIDYMA

A modern virtue, recycling was often an ancient necessity. Papyrus paper, for example, was too expensive to use once. Like our habit of taping over existing videos or cassettes, people took scrolls already filled with writing and wrote on them again, using the spaces between the lines. Even pieces of scrolls got recycled as mummy wrappings or packing material for coffins. Broken pottery served as notepaper, a place to doodle cartoons, graffiti, or a pyramid work-gang's "tag." From these unlikely places historians have uncovered thousands of powerful and intimate documents: love letters, receipts, divorce papers, oracle questions, and contracts, including one that reveals the story of wet nurse Didyma, a woman whose home turf was Alexandrian Egypt of 13 B.C.

In her times—in fact, throughout most of history—many women rented out their lactating equipment. Didyma and her colleagues sometimes worked as live-in nannies, breast-feeding and giving child care for a new mom of wealthier status. Wet-nursing could also be pure business. Rather than abortion or infanticide, parents who didn't want a newborn child "recycled" it, or tried to, by leaving it in the local temple. Whoever took the child became its owner; repugnant as it sounds to us, recycling free humans into slaves was a common practice, one of the reasons the slave labor force was so vast.

In this instance, a woman named Isadora found an exposed infant, which she planned to keep as a slave, and paid Didyma to look after its care and feeding. Her wages? Ten silver drachmas and a half-liter of oil a month (oil, the all-purpose commodity, served as soap, fuel for lamps, moisturizer, and cooking ingredient back then). Didyma had a little place in the country; she was required to bring the baby four days a month for Isadora's once-over.

Cold as the whole thing sounds, both parties cared about the well-being of the baby. Didyma had to agree to take proper care of herself and the child and to look after its personal belongings. There were standards for wet nurses—even books on the subject. The ideal nurse was clean, alert, sober, and trained in child care. Employers were sticklers—no getting pregnant or suckling another child on the job. Even if she were married, Didyma couldn't sleep with a man during her contract (hard to imagine how anyone monitored that).

Not a simple job, wet nursing. Didyma's main challenge was to make sure she could go with the flow for 16 months, because failure to perform that long meant heavy fines—more than five hundred drachmas. The contract also protected Didyma: Her employer had to deliver her monthly salary and couldn't remove the baby until the contract was up—or the five-hundred-drachma fine went to Didyma. The intimate nature of nursing makes it probable that Didyma bonded at least a bit with her small charges. Children suckled by wet nurses often grew up with intense affection for them—Alexander the Great, for instance, loved his nurse Lanice dearly. The concept of mammaries for hire might seem strange; what, then, would Didyma and company think of our twentieth-century penchant for surrogate mothers and sperm banks?

MARÍA PROPHETÍSSIMA

❖❖❖❖❖

Among her accomplishments, María Prophetíssima invented a standard prop in kitchens for 2,000 years: the double boiler. María's real love affair was with alchemy, however, not haute cuisine. The forerunner of modern chemistry, alchemy came out of a mystical quest by early scientists. They were looking for the Philosopher's Stone, a primal substance that would turn everything it touched to gold.

María had the luck to live in Alexandria of the first century A.D., a yeasty city of exploration and experimentation. She was probably a mix of Jewish, Roman, and Egyptian blood, as cosmopolitan as the city. Alchemy and Alexandria were made for each other. After millennia under the pharaohs, Egyptian artisans had fine-tuned the arts of jewelry making, glasswork, metallurgy, and ceramics. Alchemists like María borrowed the tools and processes of these highly refined arts to pursue their own ends.

Or they invented new ones, as María did. The first true still, which was to enable alchemists to "find the essence of that which is bodily, and embody that which is spirit," is credited to her. There's no evidence that this three-part apparatus helped her find the Philosopher's Stone, but it came in mighty handy for distilling perfume and other substances. María then came up with the *kerotakis*, a covered pot whose vapors could waft over gold leaf and other esoteric (and expensive) ingredients to produce the desired effect. No show on the Stone again, but now María had a double boiler, useful for making a nice egg custard to keep her spirits up after these dead ends.

These experiments and others being a bust, metaphysically speaking, María put her alchemical recipes together in a book called *The Dialogue of María and Aros on the Magistery of Hermes*. Darn thing sold, too, as did a similar volume called *The Gold-Making of Cleopatra* (not *that* Cleopatra), in which María's invention is diagrammed. A folk memory of María still exists; cooks in France and Spain, for instance, still call their double boiler *"le bain de Marie"* or *"baño-María"*—Mary's bath.

With real estate, it's always been location, location, location. In ancient Egypt, however, "prime land" was often the soggiest—like the marshes throughout the Delta region of the Nile, full of waterfowl, fishes, and stands of papyrus, the plant most in demand to make paper, boat sales, and canoes in those days. As the owner of various papyrus marshes, **Dionysia** was in the catbird seat when it came to revenue. Around 5 B.C., she leased her wetlands cash crop for a cool 5,000 silver drachmas a year, paid monthly. Woe be unto the lessees who failed to meet her terms; if the drachmas dried up, they could be evicted, arrested, and imprisoned, followed by repayment with penalties (an even tougher chore behind bars). Dionysia's desires on these points were carefully spelled out in a contract, written on the very best papyrus, of course.

PERPETUA & FELICITY

◆◆◆◆◆

For a thrill-seeker or a serious masochist, there was nothing like being an early Christian. Besides the pleasures of fasting, mortifying the body, and political persecution, you were often treated to barbaric punishments, including the Olympics of martyrdom, *ad bestias*—being thrown to the wild beasts. Perpetua, Felicity, and a huge number of other Christian women died *ad bestias*. Perpetua kept a journal while in prison, a moving—at times revolting—account in the Anne Frank tradition.

Perpetua began with good cards: a well-born Carthaginian of the Roman Empire, well-educated by loving parents—a yuppie of her times, in fact. Her dad, a staunch old boy who believed in the Roman gods and in his emperor Septimius Severus as a god, tried to talk his daughter out of her involvement with the Christians, especially the Montanist sect, with its beliefs in that women's equality thing. He flopped. In fact, twenty-two-year-old Perpetua turned around and converted her own African slave Felicity.

Politically active Perpetua also became sexually active. She may have had a husband—if so, he was nowhere in sight when the hammer came down. She definitely had an infant boy, who was with her, Felicity, and other members of their group when they got busted for proselytizing, a recent law having forbidden Christians and Jews to promote their faiths.

While she was in prison, her dad again tried to get Perpetua to save her life and her child's with little recanting. She said, "Dad, do you see this vase on the ground?"

"Of course."

"Could you call it by any name other than what it is?" When he responded no, she said, "It's the same with me. I can't call myself anything other than what I am—a Christian."

After experiencing ecstatic visions of the trials to come, and helping her slave Felicity give birth to a child in their cell, Perpetua was taken to court, where she reaffirmed her faith. Of that day, her diary says, "Then Hilarianus passed sentence on all of us: we were condemned to the beasts, and we returned to prison in high spirits." Her diary ends with a final vision and the words: "As for what happened at the contest itself, let him write of it who will."

Before dawn on March 7, A.D. 203, the two women and the other martyrs were taken, singing, to the arena, where they were stripped, then tossed and mauled by wild cows and other beasts. Before a gladiator's sword finally ended their lives, Perpetua and Felicity were allowed to give each another a Christian kiss of peace. That same day, in a spot not far from Carthage, the Roman emperor who had set their martyrdom in motion was enjoying himself at a party, celebrating the fourteenth birthday of his young son.

HYPATIA

The world's first martyr to mathematics, Hypatia started out as your basic gifted child, the cosseted only daughter of Theon, a plastic pocket protector sort who taught at the Museum in Alexandria. Besides its two libraries with half a million book scrolls, the museum had laboratories and facilities for teaching and research, where scholars lived at public expense in a parklike setting.

Like a duck after stale bread, Hypatia snapped up knowledge: science and philosophy, religion and math, poetry and the arts. As a teenager she traveled to Athens to complete her higher education at the Neoplatonist Academy with Plutarch, whose daughter Asclepigenia was not too shabby at philosophy either. Word got around about this intense and brilliant young woman; by the time Hypatia returned home, a celebrity of sorts, the museum had a job waiting. Her talent at teaching geometry, astronomy, philosophy, and math drew admiring students from around the Roman Empire—pagan and Christian alike. She also wrote commentaries on quadratic equations, conic sections, and other light reading, and loved to tinker with hydrometers and other devices to make research easier.

Hypatia became a woman of influence in intellectual and political circles, mingling easily with philosophers, students, magistrates, and royalty. The only bad luck she had, in fact, was her timing; she lived on the cusp of momentous change. Before her birth, Christianity had been made official; in A.D. 390, it became compulsory. Bishop Cyril, the religious head of Alexandria, set out to destroy pagans and their monuments alike. His instrument: a Hell's Angels band of unthinking, uncultured, unwashed Egyptian monks whose anger was racial as well as religious. In 391, they made mincemeat of the Serapeum, the temple that housed one of the museum's libraries. Gradually, this learned *and* single *and* pagan career woman moved to the top of their enemies list.

One evening in A.D. 415, Hypatia crossed paths with a mob of frenzied monks, who ripped her from her chariot, dragged her *into* the church (I guess sanctuary didn't count for pagans), and tore her to bits the hard way, using oyster shells. Still raging, they quartered her body and burned it in the plaza. With her murder, Cyril's message to pagans of the shocked city was clear. His mes-

Math whiz no match for monk mob

sage to women was even more blunt: The kingdom of heaven might have an equal sexes policy, but here on earth, women better learn their place. Unlike in the early days of Christianity, when women and their work, faith, and financial resources mattered, the Church had itself become an oyster shell.

As a Neoplatonist, Hypatia believed that we live in an imperfect copy of the ideal world. She believed in the presence of evil, but not in its eternal existence—a belief that was sorely tested by her senseless and vile death. Throughout her life, Hypatia had been hit on by suitors pressing love and marriage; to let them down gently, she always said, "As a philosopher, I'm wedded to the truth." She may have said the same thing to her murderers.

SOBEKNEFERU

In the Egyptian sands near Dashur stands a pyramid, its gleaming white lime-stone facing gone, the mudbrick ruins slowly melting like chocolate ice cream in the sun. It may be one of the few tangible pieces left of Sobekneferu, the second woman in history to become a full-on pharaoh.

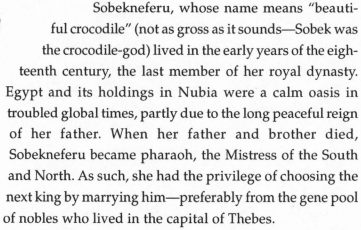

Sobekneferu, whose name means "beauti-ful crocodile" (not as gross as it sounds—Sobek was the crocodile-god) lived in the early years of the eigh-teenth century, the last member of her royal dynasty. Egypt and its holdings in Nubia were a calm oasis in troubled global times, partly due to the long peaceful reign of her father. When her father and brother died, Sobekneferu became pharaoh, the Mistress of the South and North. As such, she had the privilege of choosing the next king by marrying him—preferably from the gene pool of nobles who lived in the capital of Thebes.

But Beautiful Crocodile dug solo rule, and took her own sweet time about selection. When she did find her man, she chose a commoner from Lower Egypt. With that news, the falafel really hit the fan; Sobekneferu's love choice infuriated people so much that civil war between North and South erupted. Egyptians were so busy fighting, they didn't notice the gradual invasion of the slick Hyksos chariot-warriors, which brought local rule to a dead stop. By the time that happened, however, the Croc Pharaoh was snug in her pyramid south of Cairo.

In Egypt, many women acted as rulers or regents, but a measly four got to use the five official Pharaoh titles—the Horus name being the most important. **Twosret** was one of the four. Around 1200 B.C., she married Seti Two, who embarrassingly outlived the only heir. A born problem-solver, Twosret came up with her own candidate when hubby died—a sickly kid named Siptah. (He may have been a stepson.) Predictably, he checked out in his twenties and Twosret became the new improved Horus. Like all pharaohs, Twosret's gravest problem was her grave. Royal mummies were wrapped like piñatas with gold and small valuables, so they often got torn to bits by tomb robbers. Dried mummy also was popular for "medicinal" purposes. Despite her efforts, Twosret's mummy probably got recycled millenia ago.

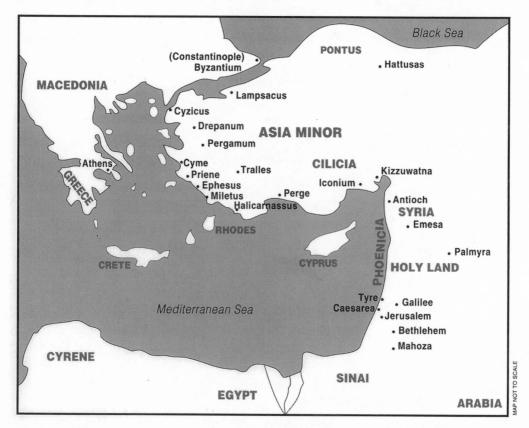

ASIA MINOR & THE HOLY LAND

TRACK STARS,
TRICKY QUEENS, TROLLOPS
&
TRUE-BLUE MARTYRS

MASTIGGA

❖❖❖❖❖

About 1400 B.C., in the land of the Hatti that would one day be called Turkey, the career field of psychology—especially for Hittite women—was booming. The Hittites had more marriage and family counselors per square inch than California. Being deeply into rituals and rites, the Hittites relied on a vast number of practitioners and priestesses who could carry out the intricate religious and magical rituals that governed every aspect of their lives. Although Hittite Affirmative Action ensured that some men did get hired, the generic job title was "Old Woman."

One such Old Woman was Mastigga, who did her thing in Kizzuwatna, a Hittite-controlled coastal town about two hundred miles from the capital city of Hattusas. Mastigga used a repertoire of psychological techniques, modern and ancient, to solve problems ranging from family quarrels to impotence. For marital conflicts, she might prepare a tongue-shaped package of mutton fat and wool and burn it over a fire while telling the couple how to let go of anger. Some of her rites were even more fun: If you felt your tension was due to your enemies, she would conduct a weekend seminar ritual to enlist helpful angels, banish your woes, or even chase your problems into the frontal lobes of people you didn't like. The props needed by Mastigga for just one ritual sound like a scavenger hunt: live mice, quantities of cord and a bowstring, loaves of bread (baked and unbaked), pine cones, six kinds of metals, wine, a tree, three colors of wool, and various live and butchered animals.

Besides personal difficulties, Mastigga and her professional peers were often called in on national issues. When a plague hit, the Hittites tended to believe that one of their gods had fallen down on the job or was neglecting them. The remedy? Get their attention with a really nice spread of goodies, then send that plague on its way by transmitting it to the correct victims, such as some non-Hittites down the road. Mastigga also served to make contracts and other documents legally binding by using the supernatural powers vested in her to swear to their authenticity.

Since currency was little used in those times, an Old Woman charged in kind and got paid in goods, the excess mice or whatever being recycled back into her practice. Luckily for us, the Hittites loved to document their actions; details about Mastigga's career, and the storehouse of knowledge she drew upon, got stored on clay tablets, a treasury of early "floppy disks" about a fascinating people.

PUDUHEPA

Royals of ancient times often arranged weddings like we order pizza—for convenience. Occasionally, however, the marriage came with extra toppings. In the case of Queen Puduhepa, her life partner gave her respect, love, and a lavish amount of legal latitude and shared power.

All of this happened around 1300 B.C.—or 3,300 years ago—in Hittite country. The Hittites ran a huge chunk of what's now called Turkey. To the south, pharaohs controlled Egypt and Nubia. The two powers jockeyed over Syria and Israel, the terrain in between. (This may have been the era of the exodus, but no one is sure.)

The daughter of a priest, Puduhepa grew to womanhood in the coastal town of Kizzuwatna. She had been a priestess for years when she married fortyish King Hattisili and went to live in Hattusas, the capital. They were to reign in tandem for twenty-four years. "Tandem" is no exaggeration; Puduhepa wasn't fobbed off on any stinking circuit of tea parties, hospital openings, and rubber-chicken dinners. The queen had a legal function to intervene in affairs of state and administer the royal properties, besides running the household. Well educated, interested in literature and Hittite history, Puduhepa carried on a busy international correspondence with her queenly counterparts in Egypt and elsewhere, and she signed the king's letters with her own royal seal. Puduhepa also avoided the mother-in-law problems of some Hittite royals. When a queen outlived her king, things got sticky, because the wife of the new king couldn't be queen until the queen dowager was dead.

Every country longs for prosperity and peace in its time, and Naptera, one of Puduhepa's daughters, became the visible symbol of that state. After years of negotiation, the Hittites and Egyptians signed a peace treaty that was crowned with the marriage of Naptera to Pharaoh Ramses Two.

The Hittite capital has yet to be uncovered; only its letters, legal and religious documents, inscriptions, and other writings on clay have come to light. They reveal that the Hittites were control freaks, with elaborate systems of wage and price control, a body of written laws, rules for social conduct, and rituals for every activity. At the same time, their letters portray a likable, human side. Take this line written by Puduhepa's husband Hattisili, in which he says about his mate: "God granted us the love of husband and wife, and we had sons and daughters."

For six centuries after Jesus, calendars continued to be local affairs. Individual Greek and Roman communities tagged each year with the name of their chief magistrate, cross-referencing a given year to bigger events, such as the Olympics. Being made chief magistrate gave enormous prestige, an office which **Plancia Magna** held around A.D. 120 in the Asia Minor city of Perge. A governor's daughter, this bright and busy woman had fingers in many pies: magistrate, priestess of Artemis, public priestess, and builder and benefactor of a magnificent entrance complex at Perge's south gate. The city walls were lined with statues of the imperial family and Plancia's own ancestors, plus three of Plancia herself. These things happened "in the year of Plancia Magna"—has a nice ring to it, doesn't it?

DEBORAH

Way back in the twelfth century B.C., Deborah doubled as both an early Golda Meir and a Moshe Dayan for the Israelites, providing political and military leadership against the dastardly Canaanites. The place was Israel, in the hills and plains north of Jerusalem. In Deborah's time, the Jews were a loose group of recently nomadic clans trying to muscle their way onto some land so they could quit being homeless. They were about as patriarchal as you could get: Females were good for begetting, and that was about it. So how the heck did Deborah get to be judge and war leader and end up with her very own song in the Bible?

She began as a prophetess or seer, a gift looked on with favor by the Jews and other ancient folks. People with second sight seemed tighter with the Almighty, making their advice more valuable. Seers often functioned as tribal leaders, which seems to have been the case with Deb. She and her husband lived on a well-traveled road between the towns of Ramah and Bethel, where local folks constantly came to her for advice and counsel.

But bigger worries loomed. The enemies who'd been pounding on the Jews for twenty years threatened to eliminate them entirely—especially that cutting-edge army of Sisera the Canaanite, whose nine hundred iron chariots and archers were making chopped liver out of the Israelite camps. Deborah's powerful skills made her a natural people's choice to become judge of Israel, a word more akin to *deliverer* or *war leader* in those days. (On the other hand, if the choice of Big D was divinely inspired, it was certainly one of God's better moves.)

Deborah got troop commitments of 10,000 men from various tribes and assigned a seasoned fighter named Barak to head the army. A keen strategist, she saw that the Canaanites had the plain below Mt. Tabor and she devised a squeeze play. Considering his hot-dog military résumé, Barak was a bit of a weenie. He said, "Not gonna go unless you go too, Deborah."

"No sweat," said Deb. "I'll lure 'em to the river; you sweep down from the north and push them to me."

The armies' arrival at the river coincided with a monster rainstorm, which made the already marshy ground a mess. Result: nine hun-

To do today: whip Canaan, write hit song.

dred chariots of fire stuck in the mud, Canaanite soldiers put to the sword, Israelites victorious. After a female ally named Jael took care of Sisera, the remaining loose end, Deborah and Barak had plenty of time to get back to the campfire, write a thirty-one-verse song, and sing it to the happy troops. "The Song of Deborah and Barak" (notice the billing) went on to become a Hit Parade evergreen in the Old Testament, sung around Jewish waterholes and campfires for millennia.

JAEL

❖❖❖❖❖

Olympics broadcasters would love Jael; they could say, "She really nailed that one," and be literally accurate. Jael, married to a Kenite, lived the life of a nomad—tending goats, avoiding tax collectors, and keeping a friendly distance from both the Canaanites and the Israelites. Alone one afternoon, she couldn't help noticing distant screams of agony and arrows hitting armor, mingled with the sounds of a storm. The next thing she knew, a bedraggled-looking soldier came up and begged a sip of water—it was General Sisera, looking like some-

Jael at tent entrance just after whacking out Sisera.

thing Deborah and the Israelites had dragged in. Thinking furiously, Jael served him munchies in her best Tupperware, saying, "Had a bad day—want to use the tent?" The general jumped at the offer and was soon snoozing, never considering that Jael might be in Deb's camp, politically speaking. Jael picked up a mallet and stake, and before you could say Smite me Sisera, nailed him through the temple. Left the tent a mess, but what price victory. Soon after, Deborah immortalized her secret sister in "The Song of Deborah and Barak."

ATHALIAH

Athaliah was the daughter of "call me a painted Phoenician harlot" Jezebel, and Ahab, king of Israel (the north half of today's Israel). The family agreed that it rankled, ruling a country so teeny, so her parents commenced match-making. Teen Athaliah soon hooked Jehoram, the king of Judah, the southern half of the Holy Land. In Old Testament style, it wasn't long before Athaliah had sons and grandsons, all of whom got names beginning with *A* or *J*. (Original, she wasn't.) When son one became king, he went to war, leaving Athaliah to run things as queen. Small-world department: He was killed in battle by Jehu—the same Israelite leader who made hush-puppies out of Jezebel, Athaliah's mother! Did Athaliah give a flying Phoenician? Heck no—she was busy seizing the throne and murdering her grandsons to have a carefree solo reign.

The next seven years were swell: As queen of Jerusalem, she romped around, rubbing out anyone with DNA from the House of David, and bringing Baal worship back into style. One small grandson got overlooked in the carnage, however, and eventually got crowned by his dead daddy's followers, who put the skids to dear old grandma at the same time. Queen Athaliah really was a class-A rotter, but look who ended up with the flaming rep—her mom.

Athaliah, run to ground and about to get run through.

"J"

Everything about her is provocative: her irony and understanding of human psychology; her gender; her identity, known only as "J" (sounds like an uppity woman in the witness protection program); and her literary achievements, which make her the earliest author of the first three books of the Old Testament: Genesis, Exodus, and Numbers. "J" isn't exactly a household word—or letter—yet. Her story began in our century, when archaeologists and scholars found very early manuscripts of Hebrew holy scriptures and classified them by age and author or editor, the earliest being "J," followed by "E," "P," and "R."

Distinguished author and scholar Harold Bloom hypothesizes that Ms. "J" lived in Israel the middle of the tenth century B.C., a golden age of literature, during the reigns of Solomon and his son Rehoboam. Of royal or noble family with the education that implies, "J" operated openly as a female writer, trading confidences and material with a male colleague, who was probably the court historian. His spicy narrative about David and Bathsheba occurs in the second book of Samuel; like his friendly rival, he wrote in a Phoenician–Old Hebrew script.

"J" wrote her works six centuries before the grand work now known as the Old Testament took shape. Cobbled together from a variety of authors of different periods, the Old Testament (and its Jewish counterpart, the Pentateuch) was reconfigured by editors through the centuries, who added, deleted, mixed, and translated with different agendas and degrees of accuracy. At times, seemingly overwhelmed with the task, a given editor threw in the towel—that's why you see more than one version of a given episode.

Rather than a religious writer, "J" is seen by scholar Bloom as an author of sophisticated virtuosity, whose high-octane talents for characterization made her stories about Moses and the strong female figures in the Bible, such as Tamar and Rebecca, unforgettable. But "J" was fated to encounter that bane of all writers, the Editor (or possibly Editors) from Hell, who revised and buried her work in a matrix of later, more acceptably pious versions. Her portrait of God—called Yahweh in her version—was uncomfortably ironic. As Bloom says, "J's lively Yahweh commences as a mischief-maker and develops into an intensely nervous leader of an unruly rabble of Wilderness wanderers."

Before you dismiss "J" as a figment of scholarly imagination, take a gander at *The Book of J,* a wonderful and mind-expanding book whose translation by David Rosenberg preserves much of the wordplay and Shakespearean-like relish with which "J" wrote.

JEZEBEL

❖❖❖❖❖

How'd you like your name to stand for "shameless, sacrilegious superslut"? That's what happened to Jezebel, the Phoenician queen of Israel.

As queens go, she wasn't that loose or wicked. In fact, it was her religious fervor (and maybe a heavy hand with the makeup) that got her into hot water. Daughter of King Ethbaal of stinking-rich Tyre, Jezebel grew up in the tug-of-war politics between the Phoenicians and the Israelites. For a short time, the nations became trading partners and political allies, and the Israelite king agreed to marry his son Ahab to Jezebel. The newlyweds built an ivory house in the Jewish capital of Samaria and started unwrapping gifts. Who says mixed marriages don't work? Bedazzled Ahab soon did whatever it took to make Jezebel happy, which to her meant a new temple to worship the rites of Baal. Ahab and the locals could handle that; in fact, some Jews thought Baal more attractive than Yahweh. (Baal worship did include several rancid practices the Jews had grown out of, including temple prostitution and child sacrifice.) Jezebel also brought 400 priestesses and 450 prophets with her, who had to be housed, fed, and given rations of incense.

This queen wasn't all take-take-take, however. When Ahab got a hankering for the vineyard next door, she didn't rest until she'd gotten it for him—by faking his seal on a document that led to the owner's convenient death by stoning. Her proselytizing, extravagant personality, and foreigner status made her the perfect Bad Example for the prophet Elijah. Elijah and Jezebel had countless run-ins: He beat her Baal boys in a public prophesy-off, claimed credit for a drought, and predicted a nasty end for her as a mongrel main course. To get some peace and quiet, Jezebel finally chased the old boy out of the country, where he died.

In middle age, Ahab was killed in battle, which encouraged Jehu, the head of the army, to jump the throne. Jehu had a few mop-up murders to do, but he finally got around to Jezebel to make the prophet faction happy. Putting on her most killer outfit, she waited at her window, mocking Jehu as an upstart. Livid, he ordered the household eunuchs to push Jez out, after which he ran over her with his chariot, leaving the cleanup to the hungry local mutts. Later, feeling bad about the dog thing, he went to retrieve her body for burial—but all the canine corps had left were the big pieces, a neatly suspicious echo of prophet Elijah's dire words.

She just wanted to have a Baal in Israel.

ELISSA

❖ ❖ ❖ ❖ ❖

The traveling salesmen of the ancient world, the Phoenicians really got around—via ship, that is. Phoenician gals got around, too. After seeing Auntie Jezebel's bad press and worse fate, her great-niece Elissa decided to manipulate people and see the world via diplomacy rather than defiance.

She soon had a chance. She and her brother Pygmalion (no, not the *My Fair Lady* one) were supposed to share power when their dad, the king of Tyre, died. Instead, brother threw an armlock on her. Elissa thought her rich priest husband Acerbas would help, but he was busy making dubious loans. This burned up Pyggy, who snuffed Acerbas and leaned on his sister for her capital.

Elissa—who had quietly outfitted a fleet of ships with some of her supporters in the meantime—loaded her gold reserves in one ship's hold, then lined the decks with sacks filled with sand. Sailing across the bay to meet her brother, she went into a fake mourning spasm for her husband, crying, "This money is tainted with your blood—take it back!" When her servants obligingly shoved the "gold" overboard, the horrified crew knew their goose was cooked with Pygmalion. Elissa suggested a new destination—the island of Cyprus—and off they went, her fleet, the crew, and her entourage of nobles—all of whom were scared squatless. Always thinking ahead, Elissa did a little shopping on Cyprus, rounding up a high priest and eighty virgins to serve the goddess Astarte and the new temple she planned to build.

But where? She ordered the ships to sail south to the coast of North Africa, at that time a wetter, richer coast thinly inhabited with local tribes. At a nice-looking promontory, Elissa saw a spot she thought she could do something with and landed to bargain with the locals. Thinking they had a live one, the locals chortled, "Sure, we'll sell you some land—but only as much as an oxhide will cover." This level of bargaining was child's play for this Phoenician sales slicker, who took a dry oxhide, cut it into teensy-weensy strips, and laid the sucker out in a huge circle that took in the hill she'd seen from the ship. *Voilá*—the beginnings of the new city of Carthage about 814 B.C.

Naturally it took years of hard work by Elissa and her descendants to turn raw land into a Phoenicia West, but it was worth it. Carthage grew to be a world power. At its peak, it ruled the Mediterranean, especially the western end of it. Only when Rome began its climb to power did Carthage lose its grip.

Elissa, sometimes called Dido by later poets from Homer to Virgil, is mostly known through their poetic melodramas about her life, the details of which are about as accurate as your average TV biodocumentary.

ARTEMISIA ONE

In the 480 B.C. war fought near Athens between the Greeks and the Persians, few on the losing Persian side came out looking good. The exception was one heroic woman, Artemisia by name, the queen of Caria. Daughter of a Cretan woman and a Carian king, Artemisia had capably run the country from her capital city of Halicarnassus ever since her father died. Caria (in southern Turkey) being at that time in the Persian political sphere, Artemisia was asked to cough up for the war effort that King Xerxes was mounting against the Greeks. Artemisia did him one better: She showed up in full battle armor with five of her own triple-decked warships and a land army to boot. She had a grown son of her own she could have sent, but evidently adventurous Art wouldn't have missed this opportunity for the world.

Round one was a naval battle off the Greek island of Euboea. Artemisia fought bravely, but the Persians took a licking. Xerxes asked her for a little Monday-morning quarterbacking, and she told him frankly that the Greeks had superiority on the sea. The king, however, chose to believe that the Persians lost because he hadn't been there to see the troops. For the second big dustup, to take place in the narrow channel between Salamis and the island of Aegina, Xerxes confidently set up a sand-chair on a cliff overlooking the water.

From her bold actions in the earlier battle, Artemisia already had a bounty price on her head from the Greeks: 10,000 drachmas for anyone who could take her alive. Right away, the Persian side had problems. Their huge fleet, too much of a good thing, couldn't maneuver or fight. Chaos reigned. The queen, chased by a Greek ship, coolly rammed and sank an ally's vessel, confusing both sides enough to let her get away. Persian losses mounted. With a sigh, Xerxes folded up his sand-chair.

Postbattle, Xerxes awarded Artemisia a suit of Greek armor ("It's perfect—I don't have anything like this in my closet"), and our assertive woman rewarded him with another bit of tactical advice for the rest of the war. It happened to coincide with Xerxes' ideas, so he thought her cleverer than ever. These days, the attorneys for NOW would have Xerxes in a headlock for his comments about Artemisia, but his fond remarks passed for compliments back then and were quoted for centuries: "My men fight like women, my women fight like men!"

Until a killjoy Roman emperor banned it, frisky females with a taste for blood, blades, and short life spans had a go at gladiatorship, fighting from amphitheaters in Asia Minor to the living rooms of emperors Caligula and Nero. **Achillia** was one. A heavyweight from Halicarnassus, known for its aggressive queens, Achillia and her bout with another female gladiator named **Amazonia** made history on a bas-relief now in the British Museum. Despite its poor career outlook, women from all ranks became gladiators. Some were war hostages or criminals. In the first century A.D., however, a shocking number were Roman noblewomen, who learned to be lethal weapons at a school near Naples. Although gal glads also fought to the death, they were often billed as novelty acts against other women, dwarves, or blacks. Like the elephant pooper-scooper, however, these dames could proclaim: "At least I'm in show biz."

ARTEMISIA TWO

Around 350 B.C., a second queen by the name of Artemisia came to rule Caria, a kingdom of mountains and beautiful shoreline opposite the Greek island of Rhodes, which it also controlled. Artemisia Two was to give new and morbid meaning to the cliché *grieving widow*. She had the misfortune to be deeply in love with her husband Mausolus, who, admittedly, was a hunk. Good looks probably ran in the family; Artemisia Two was his sister. This being Asia Minor, royal siblings were as likely to be bed partners as bitter rivals (depending on gender—but not invariably). Brother Mausolus died in her arms, of what, we don't know.

Inconsolable she may have been; helpless, she wasn't. The folks on the island of Rhodes, seeing a widow on the throne, thought: Hmmm—our chance to break loose. Attacking the capital of Halicarnassus with their fleet, the Rhodians got right down to pillaging. Meanwhile, Artemisia, who knew about the attack, ordered her hidden fleet to seize the empty ships and sailed back to Rhodes, where she had the ringleaders executed and a couple of victory monuments thrown up in her honor before dinner. Artistic even while punitive, the queen commissioned a statue of Rhodes dressed as a slave and another of herself, shown branding the new "slave" with a hot iron.

Once Artemisia had the Rhodians back under wraps, she began building. To honor Mausolus, she devised the most elaborate tomb anyone outside of the Egyptians had ever seen at that time. Sculpted and decorated by the world's greatest artists, the mausoleum immediately made the top-seven must-see list. Our art-lover made sure the monument was an eye-stopper: wedding cake-shaped,140 feet high, topped with a statue of hubby in a chariot with four horses, it measured 440 feet around the base, with every square inch painted in the bilious bright colors fashionable at the time. For the dedication, Artemisia laid out more major cash for a eulogy contest between the top orators of her day. (Eventually, her invention became generic; now any big old elaborate tomb calls itself a mausoleum.)

Besides military finesse and monument building, Artemisia had other talents. She loved the arts, the theater, and natural sciences. In fact, her interest in botany was honored with a whole family of plants which still bear her name, including sage, mugwort, and a darned good insect powder.

Within three years of Mausolus' passing, however, Artemisia died, too. Since his death, the ever-inventive widow had been passing happy hour at the mausoleum each afternoon, knocking back wine coolers made with her hubby's bones and ashes, laced with a few spices to kill the taste. Clogged arteries or poisoned pipes—not a broken heart—probably sent Artemisia on her way to a side-by-side with Mausolus.

Happy Hour at the mausoleum.

HERODIAS

Stage mothers—they're brutal. For some of their ilk, however, the whole world's a stage. That about sums up odious Herodias, who manipulated her daughter and husbands like a Muppet puppeteer. Born about the same time as Jesus of Nazareth, Jewish princess Herodias wed her uncle Herod Philip. No, that wasn't the scandalous part; it was that ambitious Herodias kept on looking for someone foxier and eventually found him in her own brother-in-law Herod Antipas. The thirtysomething noblewoman and the normally nonimpetuous prince met and melded in Rome. Antipas tried to unhitch his thirty-year marriage by mail. His Arab wife was a little upset, but nothing compared to his humiliated and vengeful father-in-law.

The lovebirds took the most heat, however, over Herodias' divorce. Jewish scriptural law really frowned on a man marrying his brother's wife while the brother was still alive. The happy couple returned to their love nest in Tiberias on the Sea of Galilee, only to find themselves at the top of the spit-list of John the Baptist, local prophet and member of the fanatical Essene sect, whose informal slogan was "Women not welcome." Rude and rabid as John was, Herod Antipas hesitated to remove him outright. John had quite a following.

Herodias, however, really hated being on the wrong end of the prophet's accusing finger. Ever the stage mama, she arranged a little dance recital for her husband's birthday party, starring her voluptuous daughter, Salome. Few amateur performances get the kind of results Salome's did. Good wine, congenial male friends, late hours, and outrageous dancing put Herod in a mellow mood. He laughingly said that Salome could have whatever she wanted as a gift. No slouch at being coached, she asked for John the Baptist's head à la carte.

Apparently, Herod disliked being laughed at as a wussy Indian-giver more than being a murderer, so Herodias got her wish for John's golden silence. Ultimately, Emperor Caligula of Rome snatched away Herod's Holy Land real estate and banished him to Gaul in A.D. 39. Herodias, true to him in her own fashion, went with him.

As for Salome, she married three times, had daughters of her own, kept her figure, and even got her portrait on the coins of Chalcis in Greece. Her fifteen minutes of fame, gruesomely tacky as they were, remain a twisted inspiration to stage mothers everywhere.

Salome receiving her take-out order: John's head on a platter.

HEDEA & SISTERS

The first century A.D. was a glory time for athletes like Hedea and her two sisters. Almost every city in the Roman Empire had public baths and a gymnasium with physical fitness facilities. Each year, three hundred major athletic games were held around the Mediterranean. Good Roman roads made land travel slow but safe, and the navy had put a stop to once-rampant piracy.

Tralles, a typically prosperous and sports-mad city overlooking the Maeander River in Asia Minor, was the hometown of this triple-threat trio. Tryphosa and Dionysia, the oldest and the baby, specialized in running. Hedea was an all-rounder. Besides track, she raced war chariots, sang, and played the lyre.

The sisters competed in two types of events: "crown" and "money." Crown games included the original Big Four—Olympian, Pythian, Isthmian and Nemean. At them, winners got high-status but symbolic crowns. Once back home, though, the perks flowed, from money to free meals for life (a lot like Olympic athletes these days). At money games, winners got cash and other gifts, paid for by the sponsoring city. First prize in the two-hundred-meter footrace, for example, could amount to four times a soldier's annual salary. Goodies aside, athletes won incredible fame. Athletic competition on the game circuit, and female participation in it, was a rapid-growth industry.

The trio's win record was astonishing. Over a period of some five years, Tryphosa took crowns at the Isthmian Games near Corinth and the next Pythian Games at Delphi—the first girl to do so. Dionysia won track firsts at the Asclepeian Festival in Epidaurus and the Nemean Games. Hedea won the war-chariot race at the Isthmian Games and two firsts for track at the Nemean and Sicyonian Games. She also nabbed a first for lyre players at the Sebasteia at Athens. These golds are only career highlights, inscribed by a proud dad on their statue base at Delphi. The formidable sisters no doubt racked up countless place and shows, but only winners got recorded or rewarded. In the status category, the sisters were made honorary citizens of Delphi, Corinth, and Athens. Citizenship (which women often lacked in certain times and places) gave such benefits as the vote, tax-free pensions, and office-holding privileges.

The sisters may not have endorsed track shoes, but they surely served as role models for girls everywhere. By the time they retired from competition, the words of a certain Paul of Tarsus, die-hard evangelist and sports fan, were on everyone's lips: "I have fought the good fight; I have finished the course; I have kept the faith." His words could just as easily have summed up the lives of the track trio from Tralles.

THECLA

In the early part of the first century A.D., a remarkable feminist named Jesus nearly broke the mold of sex roles. He loved women, respected their minds, and pushed them to grow. The early Christian movement, a loving home for women at first, was happy to accept female activism, labor, martyrdom, cash donations, and homes to use as meeting places. Soon, however, leaders arose such as Paul of Tarsus, Mr. "Better to Marry Than to Burn—but, really, it'd be best if we left out women altogether."

Oddly enough, Paul had a grimly determined female disciple named Thecla. Not that you've heard of her—she goes unmentioned in Paul's letters. (What we know of his writing, however, may not be his entire output; his letters, written between A.D. 50 and 62, disappeared for decades, surfacing in the second century to be incorporated into the scriptures.)

Thecla met Paul on his first missionary journey, when he hit Iconium, her hometown in Asia Minor (now Konya, Turkey, an inland city north of Tarsus). The young woman had leaned out her window to hear him speak and was won over. To prove herself, Thecla broke her "good catch" engagement and dedicated her maidenhood to God (a very popular thing to do in the early church). The next ten years she spent teaching, baptizing, building the church in her area, ticking off her middle-class family, and being persecuted. Paul, meanwhile, kept on converting folks and getting tossed out of cities by coalitions of angry unconverteds.

Thecla had an adventurous spirit and an itchy foot. She finally talked Paul into taking her as his sidekick in the ministry, where upon he got a buzzcut and a man's cloak, and they headed for Spain, later making the circuit of the Med clear back to Ephesus in Asia Minor. The last leg was Rome, where Paul lost his head. Although she had close calls, Thecla survived, returning to her neck of the woods and setting up the first monastery for women at Seleucia on the Turkish coast. Her group called themselves the Apotactics and enjoyed high standing for centuries, until some wet blanket called it heretical.

It's a darn shame we don't have a journal of this true grit Tonto. What remains today is a strange document called *The Acts of Paul & Thecla*, which contains a sprinkling of facts over a big heap of melodramatic fantasy about her ninety-plus years of life. For her good works, faithful sidekick Thecla did get declared a saint—and is especially reverenced among Turkish Catholics.

Ada, queen of Caria (southern Turkey), was feeling a bit ticked. Her husband-brother Hidreus had died three years back—no big loss there, but recently she'd been pushed off her throne by her snotty little brother, Pixodarus. Then she met someone in worse emotional shape: Alexander the Great, who dropped by on his conquer-the-world tour of 335 B.C. At first their relationship was business—"If you pitch Pixo and restore my rights, you've got my vote"—but Alex soon brought out the maternal in Ada. She spoiled him with affectionate gestures; she fixed him endless high-cal desserts (poor kid had been raised on water—no wonder he looked thin); to top it off, she formally adopted him. Alexander, bless his heart, soon burned down her capital city of Halicarnassus (modern Bodrum) and restored Ada to the crispy remains of her queendom.

ANTIOCHUS & FELLOW PHILANTHROPISTS

Try to imagine a world without chocolate—one of the many obstacles to happiness ancient women around the Med had to face. The dearth of desserts, voting privileges, birth-control pills, and other items made life a real challenge for females. On the other hand, many women of means worked to improve the quality of life for others. Thanks to a tradition called the liturgy, the wealthy considered it an honor to shoulder civic costs on a rotating basis for such pricey projects as supplying gymnasia and baths with costly oil, building and repairing public buildings and structures, funding drama and music festivals, outfitting naval fleets, and subsidizing feeding programs. What did women get besides a philanthropic afterglow? Public gratitude, recognition (plaques, decrees, statues, and inscriptions), and honors, from the best seats in the theater to honorary citizenship. The really cool liturgies linked your name with the year of your service. This sextet from cities throughout Asia Minor, the huge Greek-colonized area in present-day Turkey, is typical of the altruistic women of the time.

As administrator and gymnasiarch, Antiochus of Dorylaeum greased a lot of palms—with olive oil, that is, the Greek version of soap. Rather then lather, people exercised, bathed, oiled up, and scraped it off with a gadget called the *strigil*. Antiochus funded the daily flow to the tune of one-third pint per woman; in her city, women even had their own gym.

Besides the duties of being a lifetime priestess of Hera, Tata also anted up for secular pleasures, subsidizing the oil for the city's athletes and sponsoring countless banquets (with couches for all to loll upon!) for the citizens of Aphrodisias.

On occasion, this entertainment czarina imported name dancers and actors for events at her expense.

Phile of Priene became the city's first female magistrate. With her own funds, she built the first reservoir and aqueduct her city had ever seen. Phile's infrastructure was no doubt welcome in this typically Greek urban center, with its water-gobbling public baths and gym facilities.

Julia Severa lived in Acmoneia near the Black Sea. Around A.D. 60, in the reign of Nero, she was appointed city monetary magistrate. Julia must have donated a mint, because her name even got on the local coinage.

Menodora of Sillyon had already chalked up four religious and three civic posts as a liturgist when her son died. Then she turned her grief into nutritional help for the living children of her city by funding a huge feeding program. Altogether, her largesse totaled some 520,000 denarii.

Archippe, another open-handed gal from the coastal city of Cyme, was gushed over for her good deeds, which included free food and drink for every Cymian. The decrees even list the amount she spent—a bit vulgar perhaps to give the catering fees, but people liked hard numbers.

BERNICE

Sure, she was a well-heeled and stylish Jewish princess. But even with that going for her, it wasn't that easy for Bernice to see the world the way she wanted to; so in the middle of the first century A.D., she took her chronic case of wanderlust to the altar, where she found that the *Jeopardy* category she liked best to wed was called "short-lived sovereigns."

Events started off well. First husband Marcus took her to live in the exciting capital at Alexandria, Egypt, followed in short order by his funeral and a new marriage to Herod of Chalcis in Greece. Soon twice widowed, mom of two sons and barely twenty, Bernice wasn't even breathing hard. Husband number three was Polemon, whom Bernice prettily wheedled into getting himself circumcised before taking her off to scenic Cilicia, a mountainous kingdom in southeast Asia Minor (part of Armenia and Turkey).

In between husbands, Bernice pursued her hobby of dallying in another sort of lust entirely with her brother Agrippa Two. The Egyptians and the Macedonian Greeks reveled in royal sibling sex, but the brother-sister thing didn't go down well at all with the Jews. Bernice didn't care; she bivouacked with Agrippa in Caesarea, and when their palace was burnt to the ground, they tranquilly turned coats and went over to the Roman side.

That's how she met Titus, the end destination of Bernice's peripatetic love circuit. At that time a twenty-eight-year-old widower and Roman general in charge of the war against the Jews, Titus came prepared to siege the walls of Jerusalem and found his own defenses broached by a well-endowed (in every sense of the word) widow of forty-one. Titus fell righteously in love with Bernice. For thirteen years she was his mistress. Hoping for wedded bliss and, nicer yet, to be empress, Bernice kept hanging in there, visiting Rome, living in his palace, daydreaming about changing the decor.

When push came to imperial shove, though, Titus backed down. With Jerusalem a smoldering rubble and half a million Jews dead, the Romans were not about to accept a Jew, even a gorgeously turncoated one, as the next Roman empress. When Titus did become emperor, he unwillingly sent Bernice to distant Gaul for a long, long vacation, where she was reputed to have lived to seventy-two. Like her earlier mates, Titus died at forty-two, barely two years after he became emperor.

A Persian blueblood with a thing for remodels, **Apama** married General Seleucus in the mass wedding thrown by Alexander the Great in 324 B.C. After Alex's death, this pair ended up ruling with their four offspring a 1.3-million-square-mile chunk from Persia to Turkey. A real believer in buying local, Apama put her part of the world on the map, psychically speaking, by redeveloping Didyma, an oracle on the Turkish coast with a world reputation for hot predictions back to biblical days. Oracle shrines were big business, often functioning as international banks, so Apama had secular goals too. No hinky little budget refurbish here—the queen imported marble columns sixty feet high at a cool $1.5 million each. Didyma's complex included a 620-foot-long structure with seventy-eight shops and warehouses, whose rent paid for the decor of the sanctuary—a neat touch that anticipated today's shopping mall.

BABATA

❖❖❖❖❖

The Jews have had some rotten centuries through the millennia, but the years A.D. 50–150 rank right down there. First they lost autonomy and became a Roman province; then Jerusalem was sieged and ground into dust, and Emperor Hadrian built a temple of Zeus and a Roman city on its ruins. By then only a flicker of Jewish resistance remained, led by a firebrand called Simon Bar Kochba. Among his army of supporters was a sorely tried woman named Babata, ultimately a victim of the last war the Jews ever fought before being scattered for nearly 2,000 years.

Babata lived with her well-to-do father and mother in Mahoza, a village at the south end of the Dead Sea, just a hop, skip, and a jump away from Sodom and Gomorrah. People cherished the same things then as now: having a home, getting married, keeping what you made by legal means, and evading taxes. Via gift deeds, her shrewd parents gave their daughter an array of houses, courtyards, gardens, date-palm groves, and water rights while they lived. So far, so good. Then Babata married and had a son. A short time later, her husband died, leaving her more property. For reasons known only to her, Babata's son, Yeshua, got farmed out to the care of a hunchback. It was then that the lawsuits began—some filed by Babata regarding her child; others filed against her by a variety of irate relatives of her dead husband. Adding to the woe factor, Babata married again, but Mr. Sequel barely lasted past the ceremony. More hassles, this time from her stepdaughter. Soon Babata's file was starting to look like Woody Allen's.

Then war broke out, which must have seemed almost a relief to Babata, who had been fighting her own private battles. Simon Bar Kochba and his followers fought for three years; equal amounts of Roman and Jewish blood flowed. For a short while, the Jews thought they had a chance at victory. But it was not to be. Many Jews left the area; others opted to stay and hide. Babata chose refuge, an opportunity that came via her tangled marital kinship. With others, she climbed into a huge, almost inaccessible cave provisioned as a shelter, bringing a few precious belongings. There she and her companions waited, hoping the Romans would not pursue them. But they couldn't outrun thirst and starvation, even though they were reduced to eating the corpses of those who died before them.

Much later, other Jews returned to the caves, interred their bones, and neatly arranged the artifacts they had most highly valued: sandals, clothing, knives, cookware, and, believe it or not, Babata's meticulously organized legal file.

Sometimes fairy tales do come true. **Apollonis** was a lovely commoner whose cool Grace Kelly charm knocked the sandals off everyone she met. She married King Attalus I, ruler of the huge kingdom of Pergamum in Asia Minor. During a forty-year reign (269–197 B.C.), they were applauded as the ideal couple. Historians cooed over Apollonis, cities issued decrees in her honor, and poetic epigrams adorned a monument to her (still preserved in the Greek anthology). After her husband's death, she continued her close relationship with her four sons, who took turns ruling. She and the boys even visited her hometown Cyzicus together; arm in arm, she showed them the sights. Why has the shining life of Apollonis fallen through the cracks? As any film producer would tell you, there's just not enough conflict and action in true goodness.

THE FOUR JULIAS

❖❖❖❖❖

For twenty-four years, two sets of sisters—all named Julia—took turns sitting their sons on the throne of the Roman Empire while they played powerball behind it. How'd this offbeat Oedipal dynasty get its start? In a very Roman way: matching horoscopes. Severus, a general who was to be the first emperor from an African province, met the high priest of Syria while there on campaign. He also met chubby-cheeked Julia Domna, the priest's astute elder daughter, and learned not only that their horoscopes were simpatico, but that Julia's foretold she'd marry a king. Not about to argue with *The Twilight Zone*, Julia and Sevie promptly married and produced two sons. When Sevie got killed fighting in Britain, somebody had the lame idea that the two boys should be co-emperors. Within a year, the older boy, Caracalla, had murdered Geta, the younger, right in Mommy's arms. Not having Geraldo to turn to, Julia took solace in doing Caracalla's paperwork, studying philosophy, and running the empire while he campaigned with the army. Five years later, Caracalla got the ax from his right-hand officer, who jumped the throne. Julia died either at his request or from chagrin.

Soon after, her indignant younger sister, Julia Maesa, unfolded her own make-an-emperor plan. Slight handicap: she had only daughters—Julia Soaemias and Julia Mammaea. Ever flexible, she deployed her older grandson, Egalabalus, passing him off as Caracalla's bastard. The army overlooked young Eggy's fondness for female dress, declared him emperor, and off they went to Rome—the three Julias, Eggy and his sun-god gear, and the younger grandson, Alex. In three years, Julia Maesa saw that even with good backstage management, you can't make a decent emperor out of a bisexually active kid who thinks only about the sun-god and clothes, clothes, clothes. She persuaded Eggy to legally adopt his cousin Alex as his son, the first step to caesarhood. Meanwhile, the army got peeved over Eggy's naughty stunts with vestal virgins and his public requests for a sex-change operation, while the Senate fumed over his mom Julia Soaemias, who, when she wasn't busy pimping for Eggy, had elbowed her way into the ultimate males-only club as a Roman senator. To no one's amazement, in A.D. 222 mom and son became fish food in the Tiber, and cousin Alex became emperor.

Alex's mom and his grandmother Maesa vowed to keep *this* kid in line. Four years later, Grandma dies and Julia Mammaea really starts to have a ball, keeping her thumb on Alex for the rest of his life. A fan of travel and bloodshed, she loved military campaigns. Unfortunately, she wasn't very good at them, and Rome lost ground and prestige. In Germany in A.D. 235, she and Alex became fodder in their turn for yet another army coup.

EUDOXIA

Empress Eudoxia liked being spiritual leader of the people of Constantinople. It made a nice change from pregnancy (three girls and a boy in five years) and from her sluggish husband, Arcadius, emperor of the eastern half of the Roman Empire. (People said he lived the life of a jellyfish—and those were the nice comments.) There was one cloud in Eudoxia's spiritual sky: John Chrysostom, golden-tongued archbishop of the city, who was crowding in on her gig. He had the gall to say that women were fit only for procreation and spelled big trouble for anyone looking for moral advancement. When he expelled Severian, one of her pet churchmen, Eudoxia hit the roof. She rushed up to the archbishop in church, flopped baby Theo (the heir to the throne) on his lap, and said, "If you care about this little mite, you and Severian make up—pronto!" Round one to Eudoxia.

Later, she fancied a vineyard owned by a poor widow and couldn't resist seizing it. Chrysostom ("tact is *not* my middle name") jumped all over the empress, calling her a Jezebel. During the fray, the emperor kept a jellyfishlike profile, hoping the bishop/wife standoff would go away. Eudoxia got Chrysostom exiled. After his departure, however, the crowds who had once idolized her now demonstrated for him. He returned, only to be exiled again to Armenia. Eudoxia had just six months to gloat. Worn out by years of bitter words, she died in A.D. 404 of a miscarriage.

BERURIA

❖❖❖❖❖

Besides a well-oiled brain, Beruria had moral fiber: She was one of the few Jewish women to ever teach the Talmud, the massive body of commentaries on the Torah, or sacred writings of the Old Testament. A true scholar, people said she "could read three hundred traditions of three hundred masters in a winter's night." Her legal views and wise homilies were quoted in the Talmud. For instance, when villainous men antagonized her husband, Rabbi Meir, he prayed for their death. Beruria called him on it, saying, "God wants the destruction of sin, not sinners— pray for their repentance." On another occasion, their sons both died suddenly on the Sabbath; Beruria didn't tell the rabbi until it was over, so as not to grieve him on a holy day. Then she said, "Some time ago, a man left something of value in my trust; now he's called for it. Should I return it?" When Meir responded, "Of course," she showed him the two small corpses.

Beruria had to be tough to survive. She lived in second-century A.D. Palestine during the reign of Emperor Hadrian of Rome. Jews had no holy city or synagogue left, but Hadrian went further. He forbade religious rites, closed schools, and exiled or killed Jewish sages. Among his martyrs: Beruria's mother and father, Rabbi Hanania ben Teradion. She had to witness his death on a pyre of green brush, hideously drawn out by dousing the flames with water. Despite persecutions, Beruria continued her teaching. One of her husband's students, however, almost succeeded in seducing her. That incident got to Beruria in a way the previous tragedies had not, and she killed herself.

ZENOBIA

In the third century A.D., Zenobia devised a simple but elegant game plan to split the Roman Empire—at that time a vast sprawl from Spain to Armenia—like an English muffin. This politically formidable Arab queen made her home in Palmyra, a fashionable city of 150,000 in the middle of nowhere, full of colonnades and fountains, palaces and marble temples, glittering like a strobe-light mirage in the cinnamon-colored Syrian desert. Two words summed up the economic success of the City of Palms: silk and taxes. Like a well-positioned spider, Palmyra sat where key trade routes intersected, happily reselling rare goods and collecting big taxes (a privilege earned by being a buffer state between Roman and Persian Empires).

Zenobia claimed descent from one of the early Cleopatras, making her a meld of Macedonian Greek, Arab, and Aramaic blood. Although historians of old had the lazy habit of labeling all famous women as "beautiful, chaste, and clever," that may have been an understatement in Zenobia's case. She also loved to ride and hunt. Married at fourteen, she and her king had just six years together before he was mysteriously killed.

Zenobia wasn't the first vigorous Arab queen by any means. She followed dozens of early leaders such as Zabibi, Samsi, and Omm-Karja. She no doubt admired the solo life of the legendary Omm-Karja, who ran her nomad camp for queen and kids only. None of her twenty husbands was allowed to spend the night; after a quick roll in the yurt, back they went to their respective tribes. (Zenobia herself claimed to hop into bed with her husband only for procreative purposes.)

Rather than polyandry, Zenobia hungered for power. Her husband was barely cold when she marched into Egypt and took it, then conquered half of Asia Minor for an encore. Only when she declared Palmyran independence from the empire did Emperor Aurelian of Rome wake up and smell the arabica beans. At the final showdown, he beat Zenobia's forces but it took him two battles to do it. Aurelian gained more than a grudging respect for this fiery queen who could discuss philosophy in three languages.

Nevertheless, he wanted a proper homecoming triumph, so he forced her to walk through Rome in the traditional parade of prisoners and exotic beasts, Zenobia wearing

Led the parade in chain-chain-chains.

enough kilos of gold chains and manacles to sink the Titanic. (The mind boggles at what parade route conditions must have been like, following the elephants!)

Unsinkable even ankle-deep in pachyderm dung, Zenobia finessed a pension for herself instead of the traditional postparade slaughter. To top it off, she talked Aurelian into providing a villa for her and her sons near Tivoli, the world's first theme park (180 acres of daring architecture, art, lakes, and facilities for thousands, all honeycombed with underground passageways à la Disneyland for the slave service crews), where she lived in honor for years.

HELENA OF DREPANUM

At age eighty-five, Empress Helena electrified the Christian world of the fourth century A.D. and became the darling of archaeologists and travel agents everywhere by announcing she'd found a chunk of the True Cross in the Holy Land. Pointed to the site by a vision, she also uncovered some holy nails and a robe—immediately dubbed The Robe. Pretty good for a woman who began life as a barmaid's daughter in Drepanum, a burg in Asia Minor. Helena's climb from the tavern to the top began when she clicked with a Roman officer (soon to be emperor) named Constantius. They may or may not have gotten married; at any rate, after nineteen years together and the birth of son, Constantine, Constantius traded Helena in on a newer, better-connected model. What a great guy—instead of alimony or palimony, he gave her a one-way ticket to the back of beyond. During her thirteen-year banishment, Helena took up Christianity.

In A.D. 306, one of her prayers was answered: Constantius died. Better yet, when her son, Constantine, took the throne—such a good boy—he installed his mom in the comforts of Rome. When Constantine moved the capital east to Byzantium and renamed it Constantinople, he honored Mom by making her empress and putting her face on the coinage. Superdevout, Helena prayed her son would become a Christian, too. In 312, at a noon break on the day before a crucial battle, Constantine saw a vision of a cross surrounded by skywriting that said, "By this sign you shall conquer." (Those with a low miracle quotient may choose to believe it was a cruciform solar halo.) The next day, the war fizzled when a bridge collapsed, and his opponent's army with it. No dummy when it came to omens, Constantine quickly legalized Christianity throughout the Roman world and ended official persecution of the sect.

Helena, hale and happy, became its biggest promoter. Now in her seventies, she trekked to the Holy Land, becoming its first real tourist in centuries. Jerusalem, still rubble after the Romans had ground it into powder, didn't dismay Helena, who brought in her versatile demolition and construction crew. On the spot where she found the cross, she built the Church of the Holy Sepulchre. Helena then bounced down to Bethlehem to look for the site of Jesus' manger. Again, lo and behold! On that site, she built the Church of the Nativity. (Both buildings, still standing after 1,700 years, are now considered among Christianity's holiest places.)

Helena's flair for religious mysteries and church building also fired up her son, who went onto build the first Saint Peter's in Rome and other grandly pious projects. But it was Helena, Christianity's first Frommer, who had the most lasting influence. Almost single-handedly, she made Palestine into the number one pilgrimage destination for the pious, which led in later centuries to the Crusades movement.

THE MELANIES

When Melanie the Elder and her granddaughter, Melanie the Younger, went Christian, they did it up grand. Around A.D. 360, Big Mel was one of the richest women in Syria's capital city of Antioch. Joining its burgeoning Christian community, the young widow became a disciple of Rufinus, a contemporary of influential Bible scholar Jerome. Little Mel, who later inherited equal parts Christian fervor and wealth, married her rich cousin, Pinianus, which gave her a fighting chance to outdo Grandma in the "renouncing the material world" giveaway sweepstakes.

Just how much did the Melanies renounce? Between them, they owned more than 8,000 slaves, who were freed (or sold, and the money given to the Church—nice for the Church, but not quite as satisfactory for the slaves in question). Little Mel, who with her husband enjoyed an annual income of twelve *myriads* of gold (millions in our purchasing power), got rid of it all. The two women owned vast estates in Rome, other parts of Italy, North Africa, and Syria, which they sold or donated for church use. Grandma and granddaughter also threw vast sums of cash at a variety of church projects in Egypt, Palestine, Constantinople, and Antioch, endowing monasteries, feeding the poor, and spiffing up church interiors with new silk fabrics and jewels. If we have to choose a sweepstakes winner, however, it may be Little Mel; she also managed to talk her husband into renouncing sex for the rest of their lives.

Both Big and Little Mel took the Christian faith—and the different theological disputes that fumed in their day—very seriously. For instance, Big Mel helped restore unity when church wrangles turned ugly, such as the dispute over what

Saint Paul did or didn't mean about the Holy Spirit—a little dustup in Jerusalem that involved four hundred monks. Little Mel established three monasteries in Jerusalem. And after her husband died in 432, she settled down to a life of prayer and good works, such as copying out sacred scriptures in one of the convents she had established.

The word about her holiness got around, of course. Christian Empress Eudocia arrived and wanted to hang out with her in the Holy Land and go relic-ing. After the amazing relic finds made by Empress Helena in the prior century, looking for holy remnants of the saints and apostles—bones, skin, pieces of clothing—was all the rage. Wouldn't you know it, though, the two religious paraphernalia hounds got into a little spat. They both claimed to have found bits of Saint Stephen the Martyr; trouble was, they were the same bits. (Whatever happened to Christian humility? I guess Mel renounced it along with her money.) When it came to holier than thou, Little Mel wasn't about to give way to a mere empress.

GALLA PLACIDIA

The Roman Empire didn't fall like a skyscraper demolition job. It crumbled away at the edges, gnawed at by a growing number of strong barbarian tribes from the north and east, who grew better and bolder over the centuries. Other factors helped cause the cookie to crumble: double-digit inflation, lack of money in circulation, social change, and that old favorite—moral decay. The Romans tried to hold on in a number of ways, from offense and defense to appeasement, buyouts, and marital alliances. Empress Galla Placidia and other royal women of her era played a seldom-honored but key role in this morphing of the empire by blood-less means.

Born in Constantinople about A.D. 388, Galla was the daughter of Emperor Theo Two (later famous for abolishing the altogether too pagan Olympic Games). As a young child, Galla moved with brother Honorius to Milan, where he became the fumbling emperor of the western Roman Empire. Not one to see the Roman numerals on the wall, Honorius let the Visigoths get on-the-job training by working for him as provincial governors. When Galla was twenty, the Visigoths made their move. They roared into Rome, led by their king Alaric. Honorius promptly hid out in Ravenna while they sieged. In 410, the invaders finally sacked Rome good and proper—the city's first sacking in eight hundred years of existence. Imagine Galla's horror when the Visigoths scooped her up as booty, too. Taken to Visigoth central, Galla found herself a prisoner.

On the bright side, Atawulf, who took Alaric's place as barbarian in charge, took a shine to her—and she to him. Not just "me Tarzan—you Jane" oafs, the leaders knew Roman ways and may have even been lip-service Christians. Galla willingly married Atawulf at Narbonne, a city from which the Visigoths had just vacuumed the local Gauls. After a year of marriage, the Romans killed her husband. In that brief year, however, Galla had already turned him into an empire lover who had great respect for Rome and its laws—think what she could have done with more time.

Back among Latin speakers, Galla went on to marry (with considerably less grace this time) a Roman general to guarantee the succession. Honored as Augusta, her selfless strength and good mind finally got a workout about 425, when Galla's little boy, Val Three, took his booster chair to the throne. As regent, Galla ran the affairs of state for two decades, at which point a Roman opponent made an alliance with Hun forces to cut her power. She took her marbles and went home, spending the remainder of her life building beautiful churches in the cities of Rome and Ravenna.

PULCHERIA

If take-charge Pulcheria lived in our day, she'd be CEO of a Fortune 500 company. In the fifth century A.D., all she got to tackle was Byzantine palace politics, religious activism, and a forty-year career as empress and emperor manipulator. Well educated, with great language skills in Greek and Latin, she was fifteen when she became regent empress for her small brother, Theo. Pulcheria ran the eastern half of the Roman Empire at an age when most girls were thinking marriage—which brings us to her passion. This being an era when Christian women gave themselves to the church body and soul, at age fourteen Miss P decided to stay a virgin for life. With pomp and ceremony, she dedicated herself and her two sisters. (Few people noticed that she'd also provided a neat way of keeping the throne in the family—no husbands.)

Pulcheria ran brother Theo's life as efficiently as her own, keeping him focused on studies and religious duties, well away from girls and intrigue-happy palace eunuchs. Supposedly, she hand-picked a well-born Greek bride for Theo and gave her Christian instruction. Actually, ambitious aristocrats fielded a marital candidate of their own to break Pulcheria's hold on the emperor. They aced in a gal from Antioch whose qualifications included brothers hungry for political plums, air-brushed her background, renamed her Eudocia, and wed her to the laid-back Theo. She and Pulcheria butted heads from the get-go, of course. Eudocia made an immediate impact on Theo by giving him a sex life and two little girls, and she enriched the cultural life of Constantinople by honoring academics and filling the palace with literary lights.

These moves were small coinage to a major player like Pulcheria. To demonstrate her power, she put a document in front of Theo, who as usual signed without reading. The paper gave Pulcheria a gift that could be sold into slavery—Theo's wife, Eudocia! (There were a few tense moments all around before Miss P finally tore up her experiment.)

For decades, Pulcheria busied herself, making and breaking political alliances and mergers with everyone from the palace eunuchs to Pope Leo. At one point, she even got Theo to stop sleeping with his wife and go back to celibacy; they never did have a male heir. Amid a cloud of probably bogus adultery accusations, a bested Eudocia eventually slunk off to the Holy Land to relic-hunt and write bad poetry.

Pulcheria meanwhile rode herd over her circle of ascetic women, including those two sisters she'd roped into the lifelong virgin thing. Owner of many income properties, she spent much of her money on good works, including three churches to the Virgin Mary. Mary piety, which encouraged female participation, was very hot just then.

When Theo died, Pulcheria stepped into the top slot. As part of the deal, she agreed to marry a nobody general, who in turn agreed to the no-sex policy. At long last Pulcheria got to run things her way, by God, for three glorious years until her death.

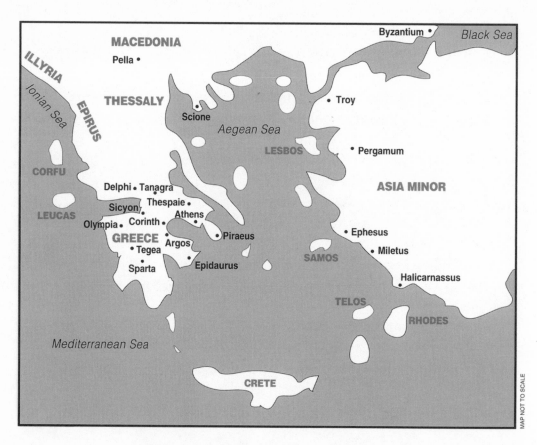

MACEDONIA
Pella •

ILLYRIA

Ionian Sea

EPIRUS

THESSALY

Scione

Aegean Sea

Byzantium •

Black Sea

• Troy

LESBOS

• Pergamum

ASIA MINOR

CORFU

Delphi • Tanagra

LEUCAS

Sicyon •

Thespaie •

Olympia •

Corinth •

Athens •

• Piraeus

• Ephesus

GREECE

Argos •

• Miletus

• Tegea

Sparta •

Epidaurus •

SAMOS

Halicarnassus

TELOS

RHODES

Mediterranean Sea

CRETE

MAP NOT TO SCALE

GREECE & THE ISLANDS

PIRATES,
POLITICIANS, PORN ARTISTS
&
PURE MAIDENS

SAPPHO

⌒⌒⌒⌒⌒

Often described as short and dark, Sappho the poet had incredible stature—both in her time and ours, 2,600 years later. Not only was her work sung, taught, and quoted—but the very phrases she coined, from "love, that loosener of limbs" to "more golden than gold," entered the Greek language and were used so much they eventually became clichés.

Besides writing poetry as blood-hot and immediate as a heartbeat, "burning Sappho" (one of her nicknames) gave life to a whole poetic and musical movement. By creating a nurturing ambience for accomplished women from Greece and Asia Minor on her home island of Lesbos, Sappho encouraged the creative careers of dozens of celebrated women and myriad uncelebrated ones. Her example spawned numerous imitators—her protégée, Damophila, for instance, who wrote and taught the young women of Pamphylia, five hundred miles east in Asia Minor.

In Sappho's day, becoming a poet meant learning to compose lyrics and melodies, singing, lyre playing, and dancing; poetry was often an after-dinner treat performed for guests. Sappho's own work echoes her belief that the divine shares human delight in beauty and sensual pleasure. Was this most famous of Lesbians gay? We'll never know definitively. The shards and fragments that remain from her nine books of poetry certainly give the impression she was a dedicated admirer of women—and a chronicler of intimate human emotions. In Sappho's day—perhaps 610 to 560 B.C.—the island of Lesbos wasn't so much a hotbed of female love as of political intrigue. Not once but twice, Sappho was banished to Sicily—

or had to flee Lesbos—for unknown causes; in all likelihood, she and her aristocratic, high-visibility family ended up on the wrong side of the political fence. Alcaeus, her Lesbian fellow poet and admirer, had the same problem.

Another mark of Sappho's stature was her appearance on coinage. Mytilene, the capital of Lesbos, proudly issued Sappho coins; some have been found that date to the third century A.D.— nine hundred years after the poet's death. Sappho (or rather, her fame) cornered the ancient equivalent of the T-shirt concession too: her portrait and name appear on vases, bronzes, and, later, much Roman art.

Although her poetry revolved around the personal, her private life was low-key and not always lucky. Her father died when she was six;

Darn! I forgot to have poet's block.

later, one of her three brothers sucked the family coffers nearly dry. (Those commissions Sappho got for wedding songs may have come in handy.) Sappho married a man named Cercolas, who left her a widow in her forties. She also had a daughter, Kleis, about whom she brags lovingly. The love affairs with the women to whom she was closest seem to have been transitory. Like many a great poet or blues singer, Sappho took the personal pain in her life and transformed it into beauty. Perhaps she was thinking of Kleis when she described her own songs as "her immortal daughters."

RHODOPIS

⊙⊙⊙⊙⊙

Along with philosophy and feta cheese, Greeks cared passionately about making a mark in this life—and being remembered by name after shuffling off to Buffalo. Few, however, carried this mania for immortality to the dazzling extremes of Rhodopis.

A slave in a seventh-century B.C. household, which included fellow slave and fable-spinner Aesop, she lived on the island of Samos. Born Doricha, she got nicknamed Rhodopis, or "Rosy Cheeks," when she was put to work as a sexual saleswoman in Naucratis, Egypt. It wasn't long before she bumped into a Lesbian wine salesman named Charaxus. (The wine was Lesbian, the traveling salesman heterosexual, or this story wouldn't have gone much further.) In no time, Charaxus was monopolizing Rosy's merchandise, who charged up to a talent (four figures in U.S. currency) a night. Utterly lovesick, he then spent a vast sum to redeem Rosy from slavery. Just how vast? Enough to nearly bankrupt his aristocratic family—which included his younger sister, the poet Sappho. But worse was in store: in the final chapter of When Rosy Met Chary, the pair got married. The happy hooker liked her line of work, however; even after the honeymoon, she refused to quit, and kept on amassing those talents.

Rosy had more than prostitution in mind. As someone who traded in soft goods (that is, herself), she longed to leave more concrete evidence of her success in life. Not content with a tasteful tombstone, Rosy dreamed of building a huge pyramid dedicated to love. Conflicting accounts make it hard to know whether her pointed ambition saw the light of day or not. Some writers claim it did; another story has it that the pyramid scheme took a dump, and Rosy decided to invest in iron spits instead, dedicating them to the gods at the prestigious shrine at Delphi. One historian said he saw them piled in a big heap behind an altar. From pyramids to barbecue spits might seem like a major downsizing; spits, however, were an early form of money in the Greek world. To add to the confusion, Greeks used the word obelisk to describe both a roasting spit and a tall, Washington monument-shaped object. Obelisks and pyramids, moreover, both had triangular tops tipped with electrum, an alloy of gold and silver that glittered sensationally in the sun.

Ironically, Rosy's longest-term fame came via her disgruntled sister-in-law, Sappho. Incredibly steamed by her brother's embarrassing relationship and the unrosy financial straits into which it put the family, she fired off various bitter poems to express her chagrin. Fragments of five have been found, including this reconstruction by poet Beram Saklatvala:

> But O Charaxus, you have chosen badly!
> Doricha can be bought by any man,
> her kisses are a merchandise for gold.
> You've taken for your joy a thing of sale,
> And joined yourself to her much-wandering love,
> And count as beautiful what all may buy!

Given her sister-in-law Rosy's cheeky bid for the limelight, a convenient case of writer's block on Sappho's part would have been a better move, don't you think?

ARISTONICE

〰〰〰〰〰

A prognosticator par excellence, Aristonice, like Dear Abby and Ann, gave advice to the power-mad, the perplexed, and the lovelorn. As one in a long line of Pythian prophetesses at the Delphic oracle, Aristonice's often-ambiguous words packed more punch than a personal note from the president, a dispensation from the Pope, or a Harris poll. There were other important oracles around the ancient world, and Delphi was tied into them via passenger pigeon service, allowing the occasional exchange of harder data to increase customer satisfaction, shall we say, in psychic accuracy.

Aristonice's career as the Pythian oracle occurred around 500 B.C. Over its long history, the requirements for the job changed. Earlier on, the Pythia had to be a young virgin, until an unfortunate incident involving a randy Thessalian, when the job specs were hastily changed to require a woman of mature years dressed like a virgin. (The well-dressed virgin of that time wore a short white dress above the knees and a purple veil over the face.) In Aristonice's time, women chosen as Pythias had to be morally pure, with good nerves and a head for heights. As the priests said and Jeanne Dixon would second, psychic service was a strenuous existence.

Besides prestige, the job had great hours; Aristonice prophesied "live" only on the seventh day of the month, nine months a year. There were tricky working conditions, however. OSHA would have shut the place down in a minute. To crank up her oracular powers, Aristonice took an icy purification bath, then watched a young goat get sprinkled with water; if it shivered, the oracle was open for business. Aristonice then sat on an iron tripod and dangled precariously above a deep chasm for hours. She may or may not have chewed laurel leaves or breathed fumes from the chasm. Those things were trappings; Aristonice was adept, a medium who had learned to use her psychic powers to the fullest, probably with the help of hypnotic suggestion and training from the other two Pythias on hand.

Aristonice gained fame for her prophesies at a critical time—just before the war between the Greeks and the Persians. Twice the Athenian delegation paid the oracle fee, only to hear her say in cryptic verses that the Greeks would take it in the shorts. She really wowed them when she said the temple roof in Athens would drip blood and its statues sweat with fear—and they did. That act, however, was show biz, not psychic power. Aristonice's pronouncement was part of a scheme cooked up by general and political leader Themistocles. By enlisting the help of the most respected oracle in Greece, he scared the Athenians into following his naval battle strategy—which gave the greatly outnumbered Greeks victory over their Persian opponents.

GORGO

Spartans were the Gary Coopers of Greece: gutsy, austere, short on talk, long on action. They even had a drawl—the Spartan hick being a stock character in Greek comedy. Around 500 B.C., however, a loquacious and well-spoken girl-child named Gorgo, daughter of King Cleomenes, became a folk hero. For centuries, her anecdotes and quotable quotes found their way into anthologies and table conversation. This Spartan Shirley Temple began throwing out one-liners at age eight. She was eavesdropping on her dad and a diplomat, who was busy lobbying him to fight a war with the Persians by offering more and more money. Gorgo put a cramp in the guy's hard-sell by piping the equivalent of, "Be careful, Pops, if you don't run this dude out of the house soon, he'll be your ruin."

At age twenty or so, Gorgo married Leonidas, a Spartan leader who would later win fame as the bravest general of the war with the Persians. Being married didn't cramp her style; Gorgo kept on being B.C.'s answer to Erma Bombeck. In spite of their reputation as lean, mean war machines, the Spartans had a provocative way of keeping marriages exciting: husbands didn't live with their wives, but with other men in the barracks. On the wedding night and thereafter, the new groom sneaked in after dark to sleep with his bride. Not only that, for her "first time," instead of a hot nightie, the bride got a buzzcut and wore a man's cloak and sandals!

Although with glib Gorgo it might have been hard to get a word in edgewise, Leonidas did fire off a couple of good lines. When he was saying good-bye as he set off to fight the Persians, Gorgo asked, "What will I do if you don't come back?"

(Clearly, she loved him; Spartan women weren't supposed to say madly mushy things like that.) He replied: "Marry a good man and bear good children."

Sure enough, Leonidas was killed defending the pass of Thermopylae with three hundred of his best men. In the aftermath, a Spartan ally in Persia, learning that King Xerxes planned to invade the rest of Greece, sent a message to warn the Spartans. To get the word through enemy lines, he took a wax-covered slate commonly used to write notes, scraped off the wax, wrote the message on wood, and put new wax over it, so the tablet appeared blank. When it got to Sparta, none of the generals could figure it out until Gorgo showed up and smart-mouthed: "Simple, folks—the message is on the mahogany."

For centuries, people believed that the women of rural Thessaly, the large mountainous region northeast of Athens, had the power to draw down the moon at will. How'd this tall tale get started? Like many legends, from a kernel of historical truth about **Aglaonice**, who may be our first woman astronomer. The intellectual daughter of King Hegeter, she studied sky-spying from the talented Chaldeans of Mesopotamia, concentrating on the eighteen-year lunar cycle they'd discovered called the Saros. During the Saros cycle, eclipses of both the moon and the sun recur in almost the same order as during the preceding cycle. When Aglaonice made her know-how public, her fellow Thessalians had superstitious fits. Seeing that logic would get her nowhere, Aglaonice acquiesced to her role as "sorceress" and opened her own predictions-to-order stand. Her eclipse calls may well have predated the 585 B.C. eclipse prediction made by Greek philosopher and sky-watcher Thales, invariably pointed to as a "first."

CALLIPATIRA

〜〜〜〜〜

Instead of Mr. GoodWrench, Greece had Callipatira—literally translated as "Mrs. GoodDaddy." She began life as Pherenike, later earning her nickname for the impudent and unusual accomplishment that made her famous. Pherenike came from the island of Rhodes, part of a family of athletes and Olympic superstars, from her dad, Diagoras, boxing winner in 464 B.C., to her brothers, who dominated boxing and pancratium (a showy mix of boxing, wrestling, and sadism) for decades. When Pherenike and husband, Callianax, had two boys who showed promise as boxers, the family began thinking: dynasty time! Sure enough, the older lad took a gold in men's boxing, and the dynasty was rolling again.

Then fate intervened—Callianax up and died. The sports-mad young widow was devastated. Bad enough to lose her mate, but her young son Pisodorus, already primed for the Ninety-Eighth Olympiad, had lost his trainer. No small technicality, either: Competitors and trainers were obliged to live at the Olympic village for several months prior, following strict rules of diet and behavior. Coming from a family of macho nonquitters, Pherenike wasn't about to let this detail stand in the way of her would-be champion. She took on the job of getting the boy qualified and in prime shape.

Under a broiling July sun, the Olympic Games of 388 B.C. opened with due ceremony. Pherenike put on trainer gear (a long robe draped a special way), grabbed a traditional long forked stick (the better to poke trainees with), and started mingling hard, oozing her way into the trainers' enclosure to watch the match. In her era, married women were forbidden to take part, even as spectators, in the Olympics; matrons who got busted were tossed over a handy cliff nearby. Not that any woman ever had been tried; to be on the safe side, however, Pherenike may have worn a false beard to blend in better.

Pisodorus competed fiercely and won his match. Shrieking with delight, his mom leaped over the barrier separating athletes from trainers. Unfortunately, her jump revealed quite a bit more than her happiness. Upon learning that the trainer was a woman and a member of an illustrious family of Olympic athletes, the judges were in a quandary. The matter was finally settled in a very Greek compromise: Pisodorus took the crown, his mom got to walk out of Olympia rather than being bounced off a cliff, and the Olympic committee passed a law that henceforth trainers as well as athletes would participate naked. Mrs. GoodDaddy had entered the record books.

More *People's Almanac* pack rat than Michener, **Pamphila** penned some thirty-three books. Both daughter and wife of scholars, she lived at Epidaurus in southern Greece, famous for its theater and health sanctuary. Besides short pieces on sexual desire and history condensations, Pamphila wrote popular miscellanies— "grab bag" style extracts, riddles, and anecdotes in a random-order encyclopedia she found pleasing. Hard to imagine when she wrote. Her house saw a stream of guests, from hubby's learned friends to an actor who hung out full-time at her dinner table. Guests who grazed in exchange for gossip and gifted gab were called "parasites" by the Greeks. Any writer rich enough to afford parasites and access to a library, as the prolific Mrs. P did, must have had other income. Consulted for centuries, only tatters from Pamphila's grab bag now remain, scattered through the equally random ramblings of other ancient literature.

ASPASIA

⟿⟿⟿⟿

Ancient Athenians were like New Yorkers: If you weren't born there, forget it. In the middle of the fifth century B.C., the world's most famous uppity woman painfully found that out. From a good family in Miletus, the talented Aspasia could have had it all at home base. Most important of the Ionian cities in Asia Minor, Miletus sat like a queen on the coast of present-day Turkey, a military and colonial power itself. Like Evita, however, Aspasia felt the lure of the Big Apple—and in her day, that meant Athens.

She came to the city as a resident alien—a status as criticized then as it is today in the U.S. Used to the social and intellectual freedom of women in Ionia, Aspasia tried living the same way in Athens. She was instantly labeled a hetaera, an elastic term meaning anything from "nonsexual companion" to "shameless hooker," depending on context.

Whether Aspasia sold it or gave it away seems beside the point. She peddled something far more dangerous—Athenians really hated it that a woman could use her brains and political acuity to gain the respect and friendship of Pericles, Socrates, and other male movers and shakers. Powerful men sought her out—not for sex, but for advice on speaking. Aspasia wasn't hurting in the physical assets department, either; Pericles, the divorced leader of Athens, adored her. Unable to marry, they lived together as man and wife and had a son, also named Pericles. Come to think of it, he treated her better than an Athenian wife: stopping at home twice a day to kiss her, discussing with her everything from philosophy to marketplace gossip, and giving her respect, love, and freedom of movement for two decades.

Gossiped about, admired, slammed, imitated, and parodied, Aspasia was oddly like the philosopher Socrates. Both had the guts to do what they thought was right. Like Socrates, Aspasia was alleged to have gone on trial for impiety. Like him, she had no wealth other than her treasurehouse of a mind (which probably proves she wasn't a hetaera, since most of them did very nicely in the financial area). Both had lives filled with tragedy and unjust criticism. For instance, Aspasia took heat for "inciting" the war of 430 against the island of Samos—on the rationale that Miletus and Samos were traditional enemies. There were also ill-natured comparisons of Aspasia to Thargelia, a courtesan from Miletus famed as a secret agent.

Between 430 and 427 B.C., a plague gutted Athens, killing one-third of its people. Aspasia survived but lost the love of her life, Pericles. Before he died, her lover was able to make their son an Athenian citizen. The boy became a general. It's just as well Aspasia didn't live to see 406 B.C., when the Athenians turned on the second Pericles and killed him.

Too much of a good thing for Athens?

ELPINICE

Snooty, intellectual, and genteelly broke, Elpinice managed to do what few Athenian women ever did—stay single past the age of fourteen, the year most girls became brides. A feminist she wasn't. She hated liberals, poor folks, and damn foreigners except for Spartans—almost anyone not of aristocratic blood, in other words. Yet she also contrived to live a life of relative independence—a feat that women of her class just didn't get to do much of in fifth-century Athens.

Naturally, she paid for her behavior. Athenians said she slept with the painter Polygnotus, who put her face into a painting commissioned for a public building. (That terrifying act of hubris is what passed for stepping over the line in her tight-lipped crowd.) Juicier gossip always circulated about her relationship with her half-brother, Cimon, political leader of the city before Pericles. She lived with him for years; but did she, you know, *live* with him? That she loved her brother is unquestioned; at least twice, she groveled on his behalf to Pericles—once when Cimon was on trial for his life. The woman didn't know the meaning of quid pro quo, either. Years later, when Pericles made his oration for the men who'd died in the war against the islanders of Samos, Elpinice nearly spit in his face: "Sure, you were brave—but you cost us valuable men fighting other Greeks in an ally city. Not like my brother, Cimon, who lost his men fighting the Persians." The "dirty foreigner" argument again. Cimon was already dead by that time, killed in a battle on Cyprus.

Elpinice played the flute—always a racy habit in a woman; she was also depicted on a vase playing her flute (first the painting, and now this!). It helps if you know that vase paintings, especially on wine goblets, were thought of as for male eyes only, since most parties were attended by only men and shady ladies. Subject matter tended to be nude and spicy, and any women depicted tended to be paid pros. Vase painters (a few of them women) didn't have a hot rep, either; the Ceramicus district, where pots were thrown, was also the sleaze district, where tricks were turned.

Notwithstanding her prickly ways and preference for the single life, Elpinice did marry. Her husband, Callias, famed as a diplomat and soldier, had money too. With this blunt and no-holds-barred woman, he probably needed his diplomacy a lot more than his drachmas.

Piping to a really different drummer

HYDNA & FELLOW HEROINES

What with wars, plagues, and political upheavals, there was always some Greek city-state or polis in a pickle. Women from all walks of life learned to rise to the crisis, however; through the centuries, they got lots of practice.

Take Hydna from Scione, who became an ace swimmer and diver like her diver dad. At a critical point in the 480 B.C. war with the Persians, she and Pop had a mission almost impossible: to cut the moorings of the Persian ships. Swimming some ten miles in a wild storm to do so, they trashed the fleet; in gratitude, statues were dedicated to them at Delphi. At the time of her marathon swim, Hydna must have been young or unmarried—the Greeks actually believed you had to be a virgin to dive! (Unless of course you were a man.)

Then we have Telesilla. Sickly as a kid, this native of Argos (near Sparta in southern Greece) was told by an oracle to get a hobby. The oracle strongly recommended music, and Telesilla became a poet (Greek poetry was normally sung, accompanied by a lyre). Poetic passion did the trick, and she became a hometown headliner. In the fifth century B.C., the army of her home city was creamed by the Spartans, who headed for downtown Argos to mop up. Telesilla meanwhile set the slaves and old geezers to guard the city walls, while she and the women put on battle gear and drove away the Spartans. Thereafter, grateful citizens threw an annual festival in which everyone cross-dressed to celebrate Telesilla's triumph.

Well-bred people sniffed at Leontium of Athens, a gal who combined her love of Epicurean philosophy with more earthy pleasures. Leontium studied daily with Epicurus in his communal garden school; after hours, she honed her sexual skills on a variety of paying lovers, including Epicurus. (Perhaps they did a trade-out.) Leontium gained fame for her witty writings, especially the learned rebuttal she laid on female-hating philosopher Theophrastus. But her finest moment was in 296 B.C., when Athens was sieged by Demetrius the City-Taker. Sieges by their nature being long, dragged-out affairs, everyone in Athens was starving to death, the Epicureans included. Leontium thought of her career counterpart, Lamia, a former flute-girl who happened to be the main squeeze of the aforesaid Demetrius, and did a little squeezing of her own. Result: She secretly obtained enough basic beans to feed her group for the duration. No food snob, Epicurus was mighty glad to see those legumes and wrote her a charming note of praise: "O lord Apollo, my dear little Leontium, with what tumultuous applause we were inspired when we read your letter."

In the fourth century B.C., a band of Pythagoreans, whose number included a very pregnant philosopher named **Timycha**, got waylaid by the soldiers of another tyrant, a Sicilian one this time. Rather than escape through a field of beans—a major taboo for them—the philosophers fought and died, except for Timycha and her husband, who had lagged behind the others. When he heard the news, the tyrant was dying to know the story behind the beans. Timycha, however, refused to tell him, finally biting off her tongue and spitting it at his feet. Mrs. T's heroic measures might seem overkill for legumes, but the principle she defended was the right to her religious beliefs, strange as they might seem to modern minds.

CYNISCA

Until Cynisca came along, "going for the gold" didn't mean Olympic endeavor—high-born Spartan women happened to own 40 percent of the real estate in Laconia. But being a land baroness bored steely minded Cynisca; she preferred to use her will and wealth to open up the Olympic Games to women. Among the Spartans, girls and young women had a longtime tradition of wrestling, running, riding horses, and bathing nude in icy rivers with the boys. Sounds groovy, but the main goal was fit mothers and healthier babies for future soldiers. Happily, the by-product of Spartan feminine fitness was a more independent female population.

Early in life, horse-happy Cynisca started breeding and training her own animals. She also began lobbying her brother, then king of Sparta, to let her enter a four-horse chariot in the Games. Most shocking of all, it seems evident that she wanted to drive the chariot herself, as Spartan women commonly did at festivals and in daily life. Whether she took the reins or hired a charioteer as some competitors did remains ambiguous. Cynisca won at least three golds in successive Olympics, entitling her to a nearly life-sized bronze statue of herself and her horses at the temples of Zeus in Olympia and Sparta. Her inscription exults: "Sparta's kings were fathers and brothers of mine; with my chariot and storming horses I, Cynisca, have won the prize, and I place my effigy here to proclaim that of all Grecian women, I first bore the crown." She deserved a good gloat. Thanks to Cynisca and the women she emboldened to follow her lead, Greek women went from *being* the prizes at athletic contests in Trojan times, to taking them.

THAIS OF ATHENS

ʕʔʕʔ

A sexual saleswoman made very good, Thais began her career as a name-brand courtesan from Athens and ended up royally by marrying her favorite flame, a general who became king of Egypt. Besides being upwardly mobile, Thais was always the life of a party. That's how she got invited to the glittering Persian palace at Persepolis, where Alexander the Great was throwing a victory bash in 330 B.C. Her date was Ptolemy, one of Alex's top generals. After a long day, drinking snow-chilled wine with any number of flute-girls, courtesans, and Macedonian party animals, Thais decided to stir things up. "Remember how King Xerxes profaned our Acropolis in Athens during the war?" she said to Alex, now drunk on his buns. (Thais, like other Greeks, had a long memory: That particular war with the Persians had occurred 150 years prior.) "It's payback time—let's torch the palace!"

Nothing like arson to jump-start a party: Everyone put on Dionysian wreaths (a Greek "anything goes" signal) and they started a conga line. Alex pulled rank and threw the first torch; Thais got to toss the second. As hosts sometimes do, Alex sobered up a bit about the whole mess and eventually ordered someone to put the fire out. Too late. The huge and magnificent palace was a four-alarmer. Archaeologists, who've found little in the palace ruins but stone and ashes, would call that a really hot party—and a memorable story of a gal who revenged her home turf with a little flameout of her own.

KORINNA & FELLOW POETS

◎◎◎◎◎

Poetry originally meant words set to music. Our word "lyric" comes from lyre, the stringed instrument often used to accompany the spoken or sung word. Greeks had a long tradition of reverence for poets such as Sappho, believing them to be used by the gods as sacred channels. Ironically, her well-deserved press (and the small number of poems left by women other than Sappho) has put other female poets, such as these three, in the shade.

Korinna of fifth century B.C. Tanagra was a contemporary of Pindar, called the best male poet in the business by Olympic Games winners who paid him big coin to write gluey poems of adulation. In the most important poets' competition, however, Korinna beat Pindar five times straight. In a graceful defeat speech, Pindar is said to have called her a pig. On another occasion, after reading her rival's myth-encrusted imagery, Korinna kindly suggested, "Try sowing with your hand, not the sack." The fragments that remain of her work have a clean, plaintive sound— no myth-smothered rhymes here.

Around 300 B.C., Anyte of Tegea in southern Greece was admired for her charming epigrams and epitaphs for animals. More important, she may have been first to make the glories of nature part of the poetic genre. Anyte's fame made her the heroine of a strange story still told five hundred years later. The tale goes that in a dream, Ascelpius, the god of healing, ordered Anyte to deliver a long-distance message to a man named Phalysius, who was going blind. Upon waking, she found a sealed wax tablet by her bed, took a sea voyage, and looked the man up. (In her day, you didn't ignore dreams or omens, especially if they had anything to do with the gods.) Opening the tablet, Phalysius, now with 20/20 vision, read a message instructing him to give Anyte 2,000 gold staters for her Good Samaritanism. Ecstatic about his sight, he laid the gold on the girl and built a sanctuary on the spot. Anyte (with, we hope, her poetic windfall) went home to write.

A haunting poet influenced by the literary movement on the island of Cos, Erinna of Telos lived only nineteen years. She wrote lyric poetry, epigrams, and a three-hundred-line poem called "The Distaff," about the childhood memories of a friend whose early death she mourns; only tatters of it and other poems exist. Erinna got high praise from other ancient poets. The writings about her make it clear that her reputation was based on merit. Perhaps more of Erinna's work will surface, so we can see and enjoy for ourselves.

Athens was a bore for well-born matrons in the fourth century B.C. Only women who were foreigners, courtesans, or the oddball aristocrat who didn't give a rodent's patoot about convention got to mingle. **Agnodice** had her own strategy—she adopted drag to become a doctor, attending medical lectures and specializing in gynecology. As touchy as people were about modesty in Agnodice's day, you'd think a female OB-GYN would corner the business. You'd be right. She soon had other doctors jealous. Predictably, they dragged her into court on a morals charge. Agnodice had to give the judge a glimpse of her own gyn, whereupon the plaintiffs did a catch-22, charging her with practicing a profession limited to men. Agnodice copped to the new charge and was acquitted. Athenians bit their lips and finally changed the law, opening the door to other female physicians.

THARGELIA & FELLOW PHILANDERERS

～⌒～⌒～

Greece had a three-tiered sex-for-pay system: Women on the lowest rung worked out of brothels run by the state and paid taxes to it as well. Often slaves, they had to identify themselves with special clothing and blonde wigs (does the expression "cheap blonde floozy" go back this far?). More pricey were trained dancers and musicians—mostly flute players. You couldn't have a decent symposium or drinking party without them, dressed in their clingy, see-through gowns. Like "clothing optional" beaches, flute-players were "sex optional" hired help. In the top bunk were the hetaerae, the power escorts: educated, highly visible, undeniably decorative women, often from good families in more liberal parts of the Greek world, such as the Ionian cities and islands off Asia Minor.

Women got into "browsing"—the slang term for hooking—for two main reasons: financial need and no choice in the matter. For hetaerae, however, life held more than clothes, money, and sex. It offered chances for intellectual and artistic pursuits, travel, love, heroism, or brazen horn-tooting, as these three Greek women exemplify.

Professionals of Venus weren't supposed to fall in love or marry, but Thargelia of Miletus kept forgetting—fourteen times, to be exact. Being from a part of Asia Minor with Persian sympathies, this much-married Mata Hari used pillow talk to sway her influential Greek husbands to see things from the Persian perspective. It worked so well that Thargelia's very name came to mean "traitor," especially to the Athenians.

Gnathaeana, who acquired a rep as the hookers' Joan Rivers, was the wit to whom everyone else was compared. She wrote what must have been a wonderful parody on the typical philosopher's book; hers was called *Rules for Dining in Company*. She and her grandma, once a hetaera too, lived in Athens until they both became "old coffins."

Pythionice didn't live as long as most hetaerae, but she had that ol' black magic. Harpalus, a general who had embezzled a fortune from Alexander the Great, loved her ardently. As the slave of a flute-girl, who in turn was the slave of another woman, Pythionice wanted to go out with a bang-up monument for eternity, or maybe two, so she got Harpy baby to build twin tombs of a grotesque size, one on the main highway between Athens and Piraeus, the second in Babylon. Pythionice's pair set Harpalus back some two hundred talents. The funeral was extra, of course. Her sorrowing man, followed by a large choir and marching band, personally escorted Pythionice to one of her Twin Peaks resting places.

Who says women can't keep secrets? Ancient history is full of courageous heroines who could—and did—keep a lid on it, even under the most trying circumstances. Take **Leaina**, an Athenian courtesan and the mistress of Aristogeiton. He made one of those unsuccessful tyrant-overthrow attempts—and we all know where that leads. He split, and girlfriend Leaina was tortured by the tyrant, who wanted names and places. When Leaina felt she just couldn't handle one more red-hot iron, she bit off her tongue to keep the hard data to herself. Around 520 B.C., the Athenians honored her with a tasteful bronze statue of a lion minus its tongue, which they set up on the Acropolis of Athens for all to admire.

LAIS ONE & TWO

இஒஒஒஒ

Athenians looking for an escort to a dinner party, a spot of cultured banter, or some high-priced sex had their own unique form of e-(rotic) mail. At the old cemetery in the picturesque garden district of Ceramicus, not-so-single white males wrote short personal ads right on the tombstones. Headliner courtesans like Lais sometimes left messages, too, indicating whom they fancied at the moment. The only drawback to this marble bulletin board was its public nature: A turn-down or a put-down soon got giggled over by everybody in Athens.

As a sexual saleswoman, Lais made the equivalent of the million-dollar club. Lais was a common name, the Cathy or Mary of her time. Since Greeks didn't bother with surnames, there does seem to have been more than one famous floozy named Lais; either that, or Lais was a centenarian who really did a volume business. (Remember Jane Fonda's watch-conscious hooker in *Klute*?)

The earlier Lais probably hailed from Corinth, the navel of the world for prostitution. She got around, of course, spending much time in Athens. Her roll call of famous lovers included Myron the sculptor, who immortalized her in marble, and Euripides the playwright, who conducted a running battle of one-liners with her.

Lais Two specialized in philosopher johns. Two months a year, she charged top drachma to make Aristippus, a well-heeled philosophical follower of Socrates, happy. At other times, she chose to sleep cheap with Diogenes, the Cynic philosopher who gave his own twist to the term homeless. He lived in a large clay jar near the agora, or marketplace. Despite the down-and-dirty lifestyle, Diogenes had his own slave named Manes. (Talk about close quarters; when Manes and Lais were in residence, that jar must have gotten pretty fetid.)

Lais modeled frequently for Apelles, the foremost painter of her time. His masterpiece of her, called *Aphrodite Rising from the Sea*, no longer exists. But we do have a rousing story about Lais' exit. It seems she fell in love with someone, followed him to Thessaly, and settled in as his wife. At last! A real relationship. But the mock marriage, or Lais' still-incredible looks, so enraged local Thessalian women that they jumped Lais while she was in the temple of Aphrodite and beat her to death with footstools.

Ancient Greece employed myriad Jeanne Dixons, the most famous being Pythia, the female oracle at Delphi, who specialized in cryptic advice about founding new colonies. In the seventh century B.C., she told a group of Spartans, led by Phalanthos and his wife **Aithra**, "Don't stop until you feel rain from a clear sky." So they cruised along the east coast of Italy, trying and failing to capture towns along the way. (Colonists usually looked for virgin territory but weren't above land grabs.) This got old fast; near the city of Tarentum (in Italy's bootheel), a depressed Phalanthos threw himself down. As comfort, Aithra did what women have done for their men since time immemorial: put his head on her knees and groomed him. Spartan men having long hair, she had quite a session. Either their predicament or the state of his scalp made Aithra gloomy, too, and she began to cry. When her husband felt her tears on his face, he understood the oracle: His wife's name meant "clear sky." He jumped up, joyfully pillaged Tarentum, tossed out its citizens—non-Greeks, so they barely counted—and a new Spartan colony was on its way, thanks to two women.

HIPPARCHIA & FELLOW PHILOSOPHERS

෩෩෩෩

Today philosophy is as dead-end a career path as you can get—unless, of course, you write a book to add to the sagging self-help shelf. In ancient times, however, philosophy was both a comfort and a natural outlet for women. The mentor system prevailed; women studied in a variety of ways, with every sort of philosopher, as this brief peek at four fascinating lives will show.

Twenty-three hundred years before the Beatles, a heretofore proper young thing named Hipparchia did it in the road. The occasion: her wedding to Crates, Athens' most popular philosopher. Instead of a bridal registry bonanza, Hipparchia got into the Cynic lifestyle, writing books of diatribes, raising two kids on beans three times a day, and engaging in outrageous behavior. (To show their disdain for convention, Cynics did things in public best left to the imagination.) A partnership of equals, Hipparchia and her mate also counseled the sick and troubled, arbitrated quarrels, and consoled the bereaved. It wasn't 100 percent beans, either. This marital tag-team worked the dinner party circuit, where Hipparchia debated with and enraged the mostly male crowd—another poke in the eye of convention.

If Greece had given MVP (Most Valuable Philosopher) awards, Arete would have snagged one. This cerebral philosopher from the Greek city-state of Cyrene in North Africa had the stats: thirty-five years of teaching, forty books to her credit, and the ultimate in-group compliment—many of her pupils were themselves philosophers. Arete learned her chops from her dad, Aristippus, who studied with Socrates but believed in pleasure as the greatest good. His daughter came to hold an egalitarian philosophy unusual for the times, dreaming of a world with neither masters nor slaves. Arete's prize pupil was her own kid, nicknamed "Mother-taught," who followed her as head of her school.

In sixth-century B.C. Crotona, a rich Greek colony on Italy's coast, Theano and her daughters lived the Pythagorean life, a modern-sounding holistic philosophy that combined healing, music, exercise, a vegetarian diet, child psychology, and mental health studies with physics, geometry, mathematics, astronomy, and other disciplines. Developed by her husband Pythagoras, the school was run by Theano at his death. A writer, thinker, and healer, Theano epitomized the sexual morality and serene appreciation for other living things that the Pythagoreans were famous for.

By 300 B.C., Epicurus had disciple groups from Athens to Lampsacus in Asia Minor (Turkey), where Themista and her husband, Leontius, lived. She was a distinguished student—maybe more. In a note that would make any philosopher's heart beat faster, mentor Epicurus wrote her: "I'm quite ready, if you don't come to see me, to spin thrice on my own axis and be propelled to any place you agree upon." Perhaps they had a metaphysical ménage à trois. At any rate, Themista named her son Epicurus, and he returned the favor by dedicating his book *Neocles* to her. Also an author, Themista was held in high esteem by Greeks and even the Christian fathers, who normally sneered at pagan philosophy and philosophers.

PHRYNE

∾∾∾∾∾

Beauty in Greek eyes was good—morally good; it had an element of the divine, they thought. If you buy into this concept, it explains Phryne's fame but does little to account for the life of a good-looking serial killer like Ted Bundy.

From a poor family in Thespaie, Phryne picked capers to earn money as a kid. Soon aware that she had more budding assets than capable caper picking, she headed for Athens to become an artists' model and part-time paid playgirl. Her silky olive skin, her dreamy-eyed face, and her figure, richly feminine yet almost innocent, made her the Marilyn Monroe of antiquity. Apelles, the city's most famous painter, could hardly wait to portray her as *Aphrodite Rising from the Waves*. Sculptors loved her even more. Praxiteles, the best sculptor of his day, carved an in-the-buff Phryne as Aphrodite—the first female statue ever shown starkers. Did this cause a commotion? You betcha. The people of Cnidos, who commissioned it, sent it back with a sniff, saying they wanted the goddess clothed. Praxiteles dedicated the statue instead to Apollo at Delphi, where it was drooled over for three centuries, until ripped off by Caligula.

Although given childish nicknames like "toad," "teary-smile," and "goldfish," there was nothing childish about Phryne's business acumen. One time Praxiteles told her to pick one of his works as a gift, but he wouldn't say which he thought was best. Just then, a servant ran up, yelling that his studio had caught fire and almost everything had been destroyed. The sculptor ran for the door, groaning that he'd die if his *Satyr and Love* had perished. Phryne told him the whole thing was a charade, and walked away with it as her gift.

Her beauty, divine or not, aroused jealousy. Once Phryne was taken to court, accused of corrupting women by organizing a club to worship a Thracian god. Luckily, she numbered an orator among her lovers, who agreed to take her case. Things weren't going that well in front of the judges, so the orator decided to play his ace by putting Phryne on the stand—topless. One sight of her breasts, and he didn't need eloquence. She was acquitted, and a good thing, too—corruption, a capital offense, carried the death penalty.

After amassing a fortune in her career, Phryne offered to rebuild the walls of Thebes, but the Thebans turned her down, just because she wanted to inscribe the wall: "Destroyed by Alexander the Great, rebuilt by Phryne the hetaera." The heck with philanthropy; Phryne put her money into dedicating another statue of herself, golden this time, at Delphi. Interestingly, one of the statues of Phryne that has survived now reposes demurely in the Vatican.

Marilyn Monroe B.C. plays love goddess

LYSIMACHE & FELLOW PRIESTESSES

꩜꩜꩜

People sometimes think of the ancient world around the Mediterranean as godless. If anything, this world enjoyed an embarrassing surplus of objects of religious veneration over the centuries, including an awesome supermarket lineup of Greek and Roman gods and goddesses; deified emperors and empresses; the women-oriented Isis cult and the bloodily male Mithras cult; plus sun worshipers, maenads, Jews, Gnostics, the Eleusinian mysteries, and the followers of the Way, a sect labeled Christian by about A.D. 300. Spiritually, there was something for every one of the fifty million souls who lived in the lands around the Mediterranean and Black Seas.

The visible representatives of the holy were often women, who carried out a wide range of religious and civic duties and were paid in money, property, and perks. As "calendar girls," their names and tenures served as chronologies. Certain priestesses had to be virgins; others were married citizens chosen for their high moral standards. Married or not, religious leaders became role models and community celebrities in their own right. The lives of these three women typified the variety of Greek religious careers.

Lysimache, who was high priestess of Athena Polias, the most important religious figure in Athens, held her office for a record sixty-four years. Married, she lived to see four generations of descendants. The comic playwright Aristophanes used her leadership qualities and her high-profile example as the model for the female lead in *Lysistrata*, his still-famous comedy of the fourth century B.C.

In the second century A.D., Melitine became a priestess of the goddess Cybele. She lived in the port city of Piraeus, where her portrait celebrating her term of office as priestess was found. A mother goddess from the east, Cybele had a huge following in Greece and Rome. Few Greek men, however, cared for the enthusiastic flagellation and self-castration that male priests and worshipers went in for in the East.

Being the priestess of Demeter Chamyne, as Archidamea was, could even get you seats on the twenty-yard line. In southern Greece, only one person got to sit in the place of honor at the Olympic Games: the priestess. Her special seat was just opposite the judges. Archidamea was also the only married woman allowed to see the Olympics. It might seem unfair that unmarried gals—from virgins to not-hardly—could attend. The matron ban, however, was followed (but barely understood) for "we've always done it that way" cultic reasons, so logic didn't enter into it.

CRATESPOLIS

∾∾∾∾∾

Spartans weren't the only women in southern Greece famous for John Wayne–style deeds. In her accomplishment-rich life, Queen Cratespolis ruled several cities in the Peloponnesus with her husband, King Alexander (no, not that Alex). Not a woman to delegate the dirty work, Cratespolis liked to be on the front lines. After Alex died, she jumped into bellicosity full-time; between 315 and 308 B.C., she commanded an army of mercenaries, whipping more cities into submission. Looking for alliances in all the wrong places, she took time out for field maneuvers with ever-randy King Demetrius, on R and R from his war nearby. Their tent diplomacy, though fun, was a political fizzle; enemy troops spotted Demetrius and he had to run for it, camouflaging his assets with an old cloak.

A beauty but no bubble-head, Cratespolis soon turned her sights elsewhere. She handed over Corinth, a tasty prize for any monarch, to Ptolemy One of Egypt in hopes of a marital merger. He was already married, but being a Macedonian and a pseudo-pharaoh to boot, he had multiple-wife options. What scuttled Cratespolis' grand plan was Ptolemy's passion for his Macedonian wife, Queen Berenice—sharp, charming, and no slouch on the battlefield herself.

TEUTA

～～～～～

Illyria in the third century B.C. didn't have much to brag about. First of all, no one quite knew where it was (just like its current counterpart, Albania!). It did boast one saving grace: its pirate industry. Everyone agreed that Illyrian pirates were far worse than anyone else's. So you can understand why Queen Teuta, the newly widowed leader of the Illyrians, really took it amiss when the Romans started whining about maritime law, passengers and crew killed or sold for slaves, and all that.

"Piracy a crime? We call it the private citizen's right to seize booty at sea without interference from his government," she proclaimed in ringing tones to the wet togas who wanted her to take measures against the jolly rogers. She did give a little: They would take pains not to injure any Roman citizens during the commission of an Illyrian act of piracy. Teuta was just trying to keep unemployment rolls down. In her day, pirates were recruited from the ranks of out-of-work mercenaries. People gotta make a living somehow was her philosophy.

Still miffed, she introduced a unique feature to Illyrian piracy. She gave "plunder away" letters to existing pirates, then assembled a large fleet and land army and sent them off with instructions to regard everything as fair game. Despite reverses, Teuta kept this up for several years, sending out another fleet of pirates in 229 B.C. to terrorize Corfu. The year after, she finally caved in and sent envoys to Rome to sign a treaty that took away all of Illyria's fun on the bounding main.

AUDATA-EURYDICE

～～～～～

Audata loved to ride, hunt, and fight in battle—the stuff any normal well-bred Illyrian girl was crazy about. A princess of Illyria, the misty, mysterious country of barbarians north of Macedonia, she married Phillip of Macedon and became his queen. Well, one of his queens. Correction: perhaps his first queen. Phillip liked making treaties via marital ties. In his forty-seven years, he crowded in at least seven wives—some simultaneously. (This was the norm for Macedonian kings; nevertheless, several of Phillip's fussier queens kicked up fiercely about it, notably Olympias, the mother of Alexander the Great.)

When she married, Audata took the Greek name of Eurydice. That was about the only Greek thing that stuck. She remained wonderfully free of sex-role stereotyping, teaching her daughter, Cynane, to ride, hunt, and fight in the good ol' Illyrian girl way. She must have been a great teacher: Cynane went on campaign with her dad and actually killed an Illyrian leader in hand-to-hand combat. Oops, the corpse was Caeria, a queen—a worthy opponent, yes, but how would mom take the news about a homegirl going down?

Audata had sons as well as a daughter, and realized that they needed more of an education, which she decided to provide. Accordingly, Audata herself learned to read and write, afterward proving to be as good a teacher of liberal arts for her sons as she had the martial arts for her daughter. Her late literacy and devotion to her children's welfare may be the deeds she was proudest of—at least that's what the inscription she left indicates: "Eurydice made to the Muses this her offering,

when she had gained her soul's desire to learn
when mother of sons grown to manhood; and
by her diligence learned letters, wherein lies
buried all our lore."

But Audata's female descendants didn't
have as much success—or maybe, come to think of
it, they did just fine by their own rights. Both became
queens of Macedon. Audata's granddaughter, named
Adea-Eurydice in her honor, also got an outdoor educa-
tion from her mother, Cynane, including instruction in warfare. After Alex the
Great's death, Cynane, one of his main heirs, hired her own army to fight the
rest of the contenders. She died on the battlefield. All set to kill or be killed in
glorious battle also, Adea got through the semifinals, only to face Olympias, the
mother of Alexander the Great. In this battle of the queens, Adea ended up
prisoner. Not even twenty, she proudly took her own life, SOP for a courageous
Illyrian warrior.

OLYMPIAS

⌒⌒⌒⌒⌒

Had Olympias, the brilliant, hagridden mother of Alexander the Great, lived in modern times, her obsessions with husband, son, slinky toys, and female rivals would no doubt have put many a psychiatrist's child through college. Red-headed, with luminous eyes that could melt a man or turn him to stone, this eighteen-year-old princess from Epirus married King Philip in 357 B.C.

Epirotes, Macedonians, and Greeks didn't have the same ideas about house-keeping as we do. When snakes showed up inside the palace, people said, "Oh, good luck!" Snakes were also handy as rat traps. So Olympia's fixation with serpents didn't seem weird per se until boas started showing up in her bed. After all, she and Phillip met as initiates at a Bacchic mystery religion festival, whose followers got happy with the gods through ecstatic dancing and reptile handling. As First Lady and main Maenad of Macedon, the teen queen passed along her snake-charming enthusiasms to the local women. Her husband could handle that; but then he found out that she kept her own bunk cool with a creepy critter or two while Phillip was off fighting. Major anti-aphrodisiac for Phillip. Although he was notorious for having other bed partners, at least they were *mammals*. As any shrink would have diagnosed, Olympias lacked an outlet for her brains and ambition. One of seven wives, she didn't get to do much except manipulate her kids and terrorize the other wives. Result: a woman whose rep for rages kept the world at arm's length. As Olympias found, snakes have lovely qualities, but they're low on solace.

PHILAENIS

⬥⬥⬥⬥⬥

Isn't it always the case—the yearbook with your dorky picture survives for decades but the love-letters get thrown out! It was the same in ancient times: we have landfill amounts of dull material from dozens of male philosophers. But what about the works of steamy writer Philaenis? A bare nothing. And a real pity, too, because she gained notoriety for writing the first illustrated book on lesbian sexual matters—in verse no less.

Philaenis lived in the fourth century B.C., a native of Leucas, an island off the west coast of Greece. She lived after Sappho of Lesbos but before the idea of calling female homosexuality "lesbian" caught on. In Philaenis' day, women who had erotic relations with each other were called tribads. Whatever you choose to call them, tribads knew how to have a good time: Philaenis had enough material to write and illustrate an entire book on sex positions. Well into the Christian era, artists made paintings of some of the more popular positions from this early *Joy of Sex*.

In general, the earthy Greeks—so quick to extol the virtues of male-male eroticism, so matter-of-fact about incest, bestiality, bigamy, and other such pastimes—were pretty tight-lipped about the notion of female-female sexuality. Lesbianism gets scant mention. Dildos, on the other hand—including dildos built for two—show up a lot on vase paintings and in comedies. Greeks also invented the baked-to-order breadstick dildo—so handy for lesbian orgies, widows, and desperate wives whose husbands were busy with teenage boys and other matters. Pure poetry, Philaenis would have called it.

LAMIA

〰〰〰〰〰

Aristotle once sniffed, "Slaves have no will—women have one but it's impotent." He obviously never ran into Lamia in downtown Athens. Talk about iron will—this woman could have bottled and sold it as a tonic. Lamia (called the Younger, to distinguish her from an earlier adventuress of the same name) began her career as a flute-girl, or auletride. Any dinner party worth its hangover had to have flute-girls, and they didn't work cheap, either. (Sex was part of their repertoire and cost extra.)

Flutemeister Lamia soon moved from Athens to wail in Alexandria, Egypt, becoming a favorite of first pharaoh Ptolemy. One day, she and his entourage were sailing to Cyprus on an Egyptian ship; before anyone quite knew what was happening, they got embroiled in a sea battle with the fleet of Demetrius of Macedonia. He captured 178 of the 180 ships; but as far as he was concerned, the Cracker Jack prize was thirtysomething Lamia. Like his dad, this twenty-two year old had a thing for flute players—and older women. Lamia in turn adored his beefy chic; Demi regularly made the sexiest man alive list. Despite intense competition from wives, mistresses, lovers, and flute maniacs, Lamia and her man remained passionate for decades.

Athenians often jeered at the pair and made puns involving Lamia's name—which also means man-eating monster. (She did have a bad habit of leaving bite marks and hickeys on Demi.) In 296 B.C., when Demetrius captured Athens, the odd couple took their revenge. Not only did they openly make love right on the sacred altar of Athena, but Demetrius taxed the Athenians 250 talents (possibly

$500,000) and gave it to Lamia "for soap," as he said. This Publishers' Clearinghouse windfall enabled Lamia to lead the life of a potentate—for the short term. All those high-calorie, high-fat, heavy-drinking orgies ultimately took their toll. After her untimely death, Demetrius dedicated a shrine to her in Athens, and for years thereafter, there were Lamia sightings in the temple, at the supermarket, and elsewhere.

By dying, Lamia lost out to long-lived Phila, Demetrius' most adoring and admirable wife. Twelve years his senior, she faithfully stuck to him for thirty-four years, whipping up cute cloaks of purple and gold to bring out the color of his eyes, besieging a city or two when need be. Only when it looked as though Demetrius had lost Macedonia and his other kingdoms did Phila finally despair and do a Dr. Kevorkian.

The first Mrs. Socrates, **Xanthippe** has become a synonym for "bitchy wife." Superstar philosopher Socrates was supposed to have said about her, "She exercises my patience, and helps me bear the injustice I experience from others." This from the guy who gave her three kids, was unemployed for fifty years, and was not only bisexual but took a second wife to boot. You'd be cranky, too. Socrates boasted that he never charged any of his well-heeled pupils a fee. Xanthippe paid instead, scrimping to live on the meager income Mr. S inherited. Despite poverty and being the butt of hubby's stories and jokes, Xanthippe stuck with him to the end—his suicide by hemlock at age seventy. She even cried. Tears of relief, perhaps?

JULIA BALBILLA

∽∽∽∽∽

Tourism hasn't changed much in 4,000 years. Travelers still complain about rooms, get hit on by greedy guides, buy tacky souvenirs, and leave graffiti. Blue-blooded Julia Balbilla was no better than the rest of us; in fact, her graffito takes the bad taste award for the most erudite desecration of a historic site.

Of noble Greek and Roman parentage, Julia had a tiny talent for poetry and a bigger one for sycophancy. She became close friends with Empress Sabina of Rome—tight enough to accompany her and Emperor Hadrian on a tour of Egypt in A.D. 130. The journey had its hassles; the emperor's boyfriend drowned in the Nile and had to come along as excess baggage until they could get him cremated. But Julia and Sabina still got to see the big draw—the "singing" Colossi of Memnon, two quake-damaged sixty-foot statues of a pharaoh near the Valley of the Kings. Each morning, the Colossi drew a crowd hoping to

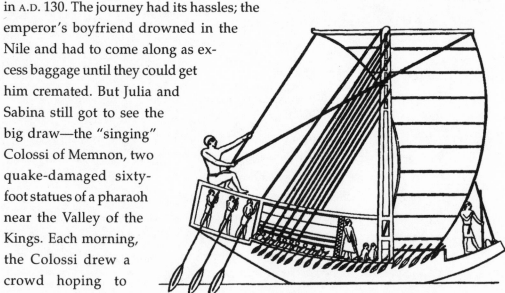

hear mythological Memnon "speak" to his mother, the dawn goddess.

Julia and Sabina finally went without the emperor, who was still bummed over his boyfriend. The statue "sang" on cue with a loud cracking noise, and Julia and the rest added their autographs to the statues. Most visitors scrawled names and dates, but our Julia wrote a sappy five-verse poem, praising Memnon, Sabina, the emperor, and herself, painstakingly written in the Greek dialect and style of Sappho, dead more than seven hundred years—a tribute to the power and longevity of female poets and Julia's expensive education.

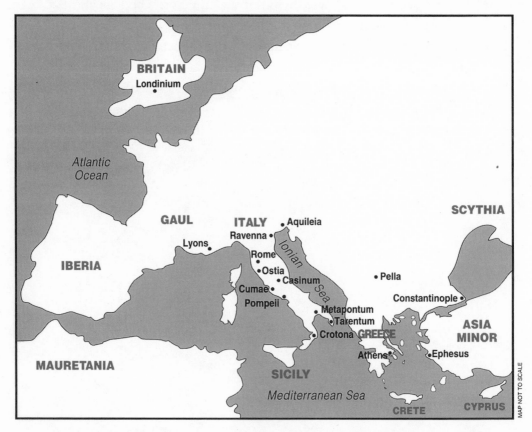

ROME & THE WESTERN PROVINCES

POISONERS,
POETS, POWER BROKERS
&
PARAGONS OF VIRTUE

TANAQUIL

✤ ✤ ✤ ✤ ✤

A dignified queen with the medicinal name of Tanaquil is one of the few Etruscans, male or female, we know anything about. Gifted in reading omens (the Etruscans were big on bird signs, making magic with amber, and gazing into animal livers), Tanaquil didn't leave much to the will of the gods. She lived in the thick of the political action in the seventh century B.C., a kingmaker for her husband, Tarquin, and her son-in-law, Tullius.

The Etruscans, who migrated from Asia Minor to Italy, occupied the Italian peninsula first. Fond of banquets, gladiatorial fights, bright colors, and wild dancing, the Etruscans were looked on with great suspicion by the Greeks and Romans, because of their tendency to include women in every aspect of life. Tanaquil's tomb didn't survive unscathed. A pity, because Etruscan women had elaborate and beautiful houselike tombs filled with vivacious murals of eating and drinking and crowned with life-sized loving portraits of themselves in their finest duds.

Tanaquil was "the good queen," so naturally there had to be a bad one: and the winner was . . . her granddaughter, Tullia. Looking at her family tree, Tullia saw her brother-in-law as most likely to succeed. Her next step was to finesse the deaths of both her husband and sister, then marry her new man and give him the chore of toppling her father off the throne. Her to-do list complete, Tullia was zipping home through Rome when her carriage stopped abruptly for a speed bump, which happened to be the bloody corpse of her father, the very late king. The spatter ruined her good gown but cool Tullia grabbed the reins from her aghast driver and kept on going, right over her old man.

Sextus, one of Tullia's sons, inherited her gentle touch. While on army duty outside Rome, Sextus and his Roman cousin were drinking, which led to arguing and betting on stupid things, such as whose wife ain't misbehavin'. They rode to their houses for a wife inspection. At Sextus' house, a typical loud Etruscan dinner party was in progress. At the cousin's house, his wife, Lucretia, was still at work, weaving with her slaves. The cousin won the bet for virtuous wifely activity. Upon seeing Lucretia at the loom, however, Sextus got the instant hots; two nights later, he came back alone for some cousinly hospitality. When Lucretia wouldn't put out, he moved to plan B: "Either sleep with me, or I'm gonna kill you and one of your male slaves, and leave him naked in your bed to give the world an eyeful tomorrow." Confronted with an impossible situation, Lucretia "chose" rape and her own plan B. The next day, after Sextus had swaggered off to camp, she rounded up her father, husband, and other trusted male relatives. Once she'd laid the detestable story on them, she pulled out a dagger and killed herself. The tragedy stunned everyone. Public anger toppled the Etruscan government, throwing Sextus, Tullia, and the rest of the overripe and tyrannical rulers out of office, and ushering in Rome's first republic.

HISPALA FECENIA

✣ ✣ ✣ ✣ ✣

Just as the French dig American culture and dump on it at the same time, the Romans of old lavishly borrowed from Greek culture while holding grave doubts about it. When it came to religion, for instance, Romans shied away from the ecstatic mystery religions and the drunken Bacchanalian cults of Greece. At the very least, they sharply criticized anyone who subscribed.

About 186 B.C., when Rome was still a republic, a young slave woman named Hispala Fecenia became an unwilling initiate into Bacchic rites at a local sanctuary, having been taken there by her owner. Hispala was no prude, but she reached her gross-out quotient that night when she had to take part in a mixed-sex gang bang of raving men and women. The Bacchic cult hadn't always been this X-rated; originally, it was a women-only cult whose festivals took place in the daytime. Somewhere along the way, a priestess named Paculla Annia had changed it into a combination Black Mass and orgy-porgy.

Not much later, Hispala's owner died and, in his will, freed her. Hispala took up courtesaning as a career, but her purse wasn't really in it. She fell for a sweet young neighbor named Aebutius and became his mistress, charging him the special "in love" rate. Unbeknownst to the lad, his step-dad had fiddled his mutual funds; to escape detection, the stepfather put pressure on the Aebutius' mother: "Get the boy involved in something depraved, like the Bacchic cult, honey, so he won't squeak about his property. Otherwise, I'll be forced to fit him for a cement overcoat."

Soon Hispala hears that her boyfriend won't be available nights for a while, because of mama's initiation plans. Horrified, Hispala tells him the Bacchic cult is like Hotel California: "You can check out anytime you like, but you can never leave." Aebutius soon has the whole juicy story out of her. He confronts his parents, who drive him out of the house. Before you know it, he and Hispala are in front of the equivalent of a Grand Jury, being interviewed by the Roman consul.

Hispala isn't any too pleased to spill her guts, being afraid of the gods and, worse yet, the Bacchic worshippers, who'd love to tear her limb from limb if she reveals their secrets. The consul promises her class-A witness protection, which turns out to be an upstairs room in the house of his mother-in-law (nepotism or what?). The whole affair goes smoother than a Mafia trial: Hispala sings like a canary, and 7,000 men and women are arrested and executed as part of the Bacchanalian conspiracy, as it was called. Instead of a firm handshake and a thank-you, the Roman Senate, it's said, awarded Hispala and Aebutius 100,000 sesterces each, an unusual and gender-free happy ending.

SIBYL OF CUMAE

✤ ✤ ✤ ✤ ✤

When it came to the paranormal, the ancient world was one big open-twenty-four-hours town. For those in poor health, shrines offered treatment while you slept, called "dream incubation." For the well-to-do, there were personal sooth-sayers and astrologers. Even the poorly heeled could afford the sliding fees of street sorcerers and oracles. At all levels of psychic service, women played a prominent part.

In the shrines of Greece and elsewhere, women who prophesied derived their powers partly from the site itself. The Romans, however, had oracle-poor soil, so another tradition developed. Every generation or so, a gifted woman with clair-voyant powers would surface. Generically called sibyls, they were rolling stones who wandered the countryside. Fortunately for oracle shoppers, they had regu-lar orbits, stopping now and then, sometimes for years. Near Naples, the shrine at Cumae boasted the Oprah of sibyls in its coastal caves. Here the Sibyl of Cumae wrote her chilling prophesies on leaves.

Unlike the Pythia at Delphi, the sibyl's predictions often focused on events far into the future. Early on, some thoughtful soul began to document them; pretty soon an encyclopedia-sized stack of prophesies called the Sibylline Books were stored under a temple in Rome. Only fifteen priests were allowed to peek at this growing hits-and-misses list—and that only in cases of dire national emergency, such as war, famine, or the appearance of a hermaphrodite (I'm not making this up—ask the sibyl).

CORNELIA

✥ ✥ ✥ ✥ ✥

Later Romans loved to point to Cornelia as the pluperfect wife-'n'-mother, the Carol Brady of their particular Bunch. The austere and moral times of the Roman republic were the good ol' days, which she epitomized. From 100 B.C. on, that's all they harped on: Cornelia, Cornelia, Cornelia. It was enough to make a vestal virgin gag.

Although her dad was a superstar general who wiped out Carthage, Cornelia didn't fret about pedigree. Over protests, she married rich but plebeian Sempronius Gracchus and had twelve children; only three survived childhood. Cornelia herself became a young widow. King Ptolemy of Egypt tried to talk her into remarriage, but our Cornelia had priorities. Superbly educated and a fine writer, as her letters attest, she took personal control of educating her own kids. To round out the boys' education, she brought in Greek philosophers to guest-lecture. Her daughter, Sempronia, eventually married a national hero. Her sons, however, brought up as political idealists in the Greek mold, died of mob violence, trying to bring about social reform for the landless and poor. "Mother of the Gracchi boys" she was invariably labeled. After she was safely in her tomb, however, political opportunists used Cornelia, quoting letters she supposedly wrote to her sons, denouncing their revolutionary activities. Cornelia became a simpering symbol, put on a pedestal for things she didn't espouse and for reasons she really would have hated.

HORTENSIA

✣ ✣ ✣ ✣ ✣

Death and taxes were as inevitable and unwelcome in Roman days as in ours; at times, women felt the sting of the latter as much as the former. In 42 B.C., five men dragged the entire country into a civil war—always a pricey activity, even before helicopters and SCUD missiles were invented. To fund the venture, the ruling triumvirs decided to slam a tax on women—and only women—whose wealth exceeded 100,000 denarii. A total of 1,400 females were told to cough up one year's income and, by the way, to lend the government one-fiftieth of their property at interest. To ensure compliance, rewards were offered to informers, free or slave about ladies who, shall we say, underreported. At other crisis points in Roman history, matrons with bucks had given generously. This time, however, circumstances were different: This was a civil war, and the squeeze was put solely on women of wealth.

Although she'd never been allowed to plead law cases, Hortensia, the daughter of Rome's top orator and legal advocate, Hortensius, had a superb education and real talent for the law and forensics. She was chosen by the crowd of 1,400 livid women to act as their spokeswoman. No male had the nerve or interest to plead their case. Hortensia at the head, the women made a noisy political march through the streets of Rome to the Forum, where she gave an enormously effective speech on their behalf.

How good was Hortensia? The proof was in the pleading. She convinced the irate triumvirs to reduce the number of women being taxed from 1,400 to 400. More critical, they decreed that the new tax would, like rain, fall equally on women and men, citizens and strangers alike. Granted, that's not as good as blowing off the whole idea, but those military boys really needed mad money.

Hortensia's speech entered Roman history, where little boys (and, we hope, little girls) read it and memorized it for centuries. By the way, Hortensia's pop and mentor didn't get to witness her eloquent hour in the sun; he had died eight years earlier. Ironically, none of Hortensia's children followed in her or her father's footsteps.

A member of the shady women's network, **Asellina** ran a cathouse and greasy spoon in Pompeii. Outside her joint, a stone sign with four phalluses and a dice cup let passersby know that the first floor had booze and gambling; the second story, the easy but not necessarily cheap ladies. An international house of hookery, Asellina's echoed the cosmopolitan nature of the Roman world in the first century A.D. The waitresses (who may have doubled as hookers, or vice versa) came from Greece, North Africa, and Crete. How do we know this? The tavern walls were covered with their names and lusty quotes about the daily specials, and graffiti from the regulars, such as December and good old Scordopordonicus, or "Garlic Fart." Although Asellina's ladies were slaves for the most part, they took an active role in politics by decorating her building with candidates' slogans, urging the thirsty male electorate to vote. Darned near every Pompeiian, Asellina included, got into local politicking. Only the candidates themselves stayed blessedly quiet—not a sound bite in the bunch!

MUSA

✛ ✛ ✛ ✛ ✛

Musa's career ladder began on the bottom rung—as a slave in a first-century B.C. Roman household, possibly as Julius Caesar's own property. Whatever his other shortcomings, Julius had a kinder heart than most slaveowners (which was almost everybody, really). He once went to dinner at the house of a brute named Pollio, whose slave accidentally broke a crystal cup. Enraged, Pollio ordered the boy to be tossed as fish food into a pond of huge lamprey eels. The boy ran to Caesar, begging for death in some less ghastly fashion. Julius responded by freeing the boy, filling in the fatal pond, and having the rest of Pollio's crystal cups smashed in his presence.

Slaves truly had it tough: They could be beaten, branded for running away, sexually used and abused, tortured if their testimony were needed for legal reasons, and forced to do dirty, dangerous work of all sorts. In later centuries, slaves actually did serve as fish food on one occasion: Emperor Egalabalus loved a dish of conger eels that were fattened on Christian slaves.

Many factors kept slave numbers replenished throughout ancient times, including piracy, prisoners of war, poverty, babies left as foundlings, and babies born of other slaves. On the bright side, slaves sometimes got chances to better their positions and become free. Owners often freed them in their wills, or earlier; slaves could also freelance and buy their way out of servitude. Freedmen and -women in Roman, Persian, and Mesopotamian societies traditionally filled the bureaucratic ranks and regularly held posts at the highest management levels.

As a young slave, Musa had obvious physical assets in her résumé. Her appearance motivated Julius Caesar to pick her as a "Hello, welcome to Rome" present for visiting potentate Phraates Four. This old gent from the kingdom of Parthia (now northeast Iran) was in town to schmooze Julius about his new status as a vassal state beholden to the Roman Empire.

By the time he got his door prize back home, Phraates had already jumped Musa a notch or two up the ladder. She became chief concubine, then legal wife, then mother of his son, Phraataces. King Phraates had a gaggle of other legit sons already, but, by and by, Musa got them out of the way with her suggestion: "Honey, let's send *your* boys to Rome as pledges of your fidelity." Coming from a long line of parricides himself, it couldn't have been a major shock to King Phraates when Musa and son went into murder mode and duly dusted him. To protect her investment, Musa then married her own son, becoming joint ruler of Parthia—no glass ceiling in this corporation— and getting some great portraits of herself on mother-son coins. In Musa's day, people got ahead by cutthroat tactics that were literal rather than corporate—I guess that makes her a yummy (young, upwardly mobile murderer) instead of a yuppie.

FULVIA

✤ ✤ ✤ ✤ ✤

It's unlikely you've heard of Fulvia—a decadent dazzler whose speed at running through denarii and husbands (Mark Antony among them) even got the attention of blasé Romans. Like other precelebrity mates, her doings have been overshadowed by the headliner who followed in her marital footsteps—Cleopatra Seven.

Mark Antony was mate number three for Fulvia. When younger, her prior hubby, Curio, had been intimate friends with Mark Antony. *Really* intimate friends; Curio's dad had gone ballistic at their heavy homosexual relationship—and Mark's attempts to squeegee six million sesterces out of his lover.

Fulvia and Mark Antony had other things in common besides Curio: They loved money, parties, and power, even if it meant stirring up revolt, wars, or trouble. When Julius Caesar died, Mark Antony had the inside track to the top. First he and Fulvia freshened up their respective fortunes by dipping into the money Julius Caesar had left him. Then they sucked the state funds dry and started selling state assets. Fulvia and Antony's bargain barn became known as one-stop shopping for titles, privileges, estates—even towns. Naturally, these gross abuses led to purges, vendettas, and wars—this was Italy, after all. Among those murdered was the famous orator Cicero, who said so many naughty things about Mark that Fulvia stuck a pin through his tongue when an assassin delivered his head to her.

Speaking of sticking: Never a man to stick to one wife, lover, or gender, Mark Antony got even busier from 42 B.C. on, commuting to and from Fulvia and family to new lover Cleopatra in Egypt. Fulvia kept busy waging a small war against Octavian on Mark's behalf—partly as a "Come back home to Mama" ploy, and partly to let her husband know that the big action still lay in Rome. Eventually, she lost and fled to Athens, where she and Mark had an acrimonious meeting before he squared off to fight in Italy. Worn out by these endeavors (it's not easy being this bad), Fulvia died of illness in 40 B.C. Ever the gallant, brand-new widower Mark fed his opponent Octavian the story that Fulvia was to blame for the whole messy business. Octavian, who happened to have a newly widowed sister of his own moping around, responded, "I'll buy that, if you buy this." End result: Mark Antony took on a new wife, Octavia, right about the moment Cleopatra was giving birth to Mark Antony's twins. Competing with a life this monumentally messy, is it any wonder that Fulvia got lost in the cracks?

Pompeii may not have boasted credit cards or car rebates, but it had money-lenders of the most rapacious sort. **Faustilla** was one who gained a certain dark prominence for her hard-nosed business dealings. Lenders of the worst kind like Faustilla worked out of gaming dens or taverns, often using the walls in lieu of paper documents. Faustilla hung out at several dens in rotation, so her transactions appear on various walls around town. Typical of a day's work are loans she made of fifteen and twenty denarii. She charged monthly interest, which ran a cool 45 percent per year. No slouch in the collateral department, Faustilla collected earrings, a clock, and a hood from one desperate female client as security against her loan. These details were duly noted on walls that survived the destruction of Pompeii in A.D. 79, proving that loan sharks really do live forever.

SULPICIA

✤ ✤ ✤ ✤ ✤

As wordy as Romans were, they weren't that keen on poetry. Even if they had been, their poets wouldn't have gotten paid. Unlike Greece, where poets openly accepted payment, Romans shuddered at paid labor of any kind—even something as rarefied as composing verse. Italian versifiers lived off their own wealth—or their families. Of course, there wasn't the pressure to publish, to produce, to be a financially contributing member of society in Sulpicia's times, the way there is now.

Having a patron was critical nevertheless for a creative person like Sulpicia, who lived about 15 B.C. The benefits of the patron/poet relationship flowed in both directions: to the patron, the hint of immortality through the work of the artist; to the artist, a variety of contacts, honors, commissions, and noncash gifts (property, favors—anything but filthy lucre) via the promotion and prestige of the patron.

Sulpicia's patron, Marcus Messalla, himself an orator and historian, supported a whole stable of poets, including Tibullus, Lygdamus, and Ovid, author of the naughty and notorious *The Arts of Love*. Messalla was probably Sulpicia's uncle and maybe her guardian as well. If so, she was bound to have given her uncle gray hairs; in her twenties by the sound of it, upper-class, unmarried and living in his house, she still managed to carry on a red-hot love affair, which she then wrote poetry about.

Other than giving her lover a pseudonym, Sulpicia didn't hold back much. A piquant and individual female mind, she's almost the only first-hand literary voice of a woman we possess from ancient Rome. (That in itself is a melancholy statement.)

To date, only six small poems have come to light; yet she packs as much fire-power and truth into her few lines as the haiku masters of Japan do. Vulnerable, exultant, sassy, bitter, intimate, and honest, she wrote about her affair with "Cerinthus" from first kiss to losing her virginity, from the shout-it-from-the-roof-tops rapture of new love to the wrenching discovery about another woman. Roman women no doubt did and felt these same things, but only Sulpicia left us white-hot, tantalizing lines such as these:

> Do you feel any sense of dutiful concern, Cerinthus,
> for your girl,
> now that a fever wracks my tired limbs?
> I wouldn't want to triumph over sad diseases
> unless I thought you also wished me to.
> For what good will it do me to triumph over disease,
> if you can bear my troubles with an unfeeling heart?

MESSALINA

✤ ✤ ✤ ✤ ✤

It was A.D. 48, but most of the fifty million people living in the empire thought of it as the reign of Roman Emperor Claudius of Rome. Some nicknamed it "the reign of Empress Messalina." Messalina's domination of the craven yet good-humored emperor, her sexual excesses, and her campaign to legalize polyandry were on everyone's lips. Although women had a voice in marital and other matters, few took to her idea. "Can you imagine putting up with more than one husband?" they snickered.

A radiant fourteen year old when she married her forty-eight-year-old cousin Claudius, Messalina overlooked his physical problems (besides lameness and a facial tic, he drooled) and produced two boys before her sexual itch kicked in. The emperor, notwithstanding his warm and fuzzy portrayal by Sir Derek Jacobi in the BBC film series *I, Claudius,* had a few habits that couldn't have helped the marriage: He loved gambling, other women, drinking to excess, and blood—from cheering on gladiatorial gore to gobbling rare roast beef.

Messalina racked up many lovers; in this, she was no worse than others of her social class. However, she did have an unattractive quirk of ordering up death contracts for ex-lovers and rivals. Oh, and yes, she *may* have moonlighted at a local brothel, calling herself "Lycisca" and wearing a blonde wig and golden pasties. Rome had no penalty for slander, so possibly that later tale was vicious gossip—or understatement.

Where Messalina really got her cute twenty-three-year-old booty in a wringer was over her public, and bigamous, marriage to a noble named Silius. The affair had a harvest theme: wine-stomping, matching animal skins for the bridesmaids, a Dionysius outfit for the groom, and a dinner for friends; entertainment was courtesy of the new Mr. and Mrs., who climbed onto their couch and consummated their vows for the guests. With their usual efficiency, the freedmen who worked as Emperor Claudius' top executives quickly took care of Messalina's wedding party by terminating bride, groom, and accomplices. Claudius' notorious absentmindedness probably proved a blessing; when given the news of her death, he was at the dinner table—and went on putting away the groceries. The emperor never did show any overt signs of grief or anger over Messalina, apparently ignoring both the tears of his little boys and the gloating of her detractors. Inside, he may have grieved for his silly, utterly entrancing wife, but acting the ignorant old fool had let him see fifty-seven birthdays. In his murderous family, that was no mean feat.

First-century Rome reeked of bureaucracy. Just to become a meretrix, or public whore, you had to apply to an aedile, or cop. After giving your name, hooker handle, place of birth, age, and what you intended to charge, you got a free morality lecture and were added to the official roll call of shady ladies. Despite the paperwork, it sounded like fun to **Vestilia**. From a middle-class family and a Mrs. already, Vestilia showed up at the aediles, demanding a license. (The registration was for tax reasons—the state collected a per-embrace surcharge.) But the squalors of meretrixing were not to be for Vee; outrage at conduct unbecoming a matron got her banished to a tiny Greek island, Cyclades—where it's safe to say there were few takers, paying or not.

AGRIPPINA

✠ ✠ ✠ ✠ ✠

Claros, an oracle on the Turkish coast overlooking the Greek island of Samos, doesn't ring any bells today. In Agrippina the Younger's time, it sure did. In A.D. 18, the oracle predicted that Germanicus, popular military celebrity and Agrippina's dad, would be dead within a year. He was, and Claros' stock shot sky-high.

Thirty years later, when Agrippina was twice married and divorced, and her uncle Emperor Claudius was shopping for his third wife, Claros came into the picture again. Roman gamblers said the empress race was neck and neck between Agrippina and Lollia Paulina, a consul's daughter. Lollia made a quick trip to ask the oracle who would survive the cut. Not only was the oracle wrong, wrong, wrong, but the victor made a cut of her own. Claudius chose to wed Agrippina, who celebrated by forcing Lollia to commit suicide with the classic Roman short-sword.

Agrippina Junior had her own crosses to bear, of course. Her highly principled, fiery mother was the "good" Agrippina the Elder, always a hard act to follow. Then there was brother Caligula, who had insisted on sleeping with her and her sisters; she paid him back for the incest trauma by taking part in an unsuccessful conspiracy against him, for which she was exiled. Worst of all, in her first marriage Agrippina had birthed a four-letter word spelled Nero. Even the kid's father warned, "Any child of ours is bound to become a public danger."

Agrippina the Younger didn't see it that way, however. A year after her nuptials, she nagged Claudius into adopting her teen cherub, even though there was an heir. The emperor gave in, guaranteeing his (and his heir's) early exit from the land of the living.

High-strung Agrippina now had her heart's desire: a seventeen year old who ruled. They went everywhere together; Nero used the phrase "the best of mothers" as a password for his guards. Agrippina Junior loved the imperial mom stuff, even if her son did try to jump her bones now and then. Well aware of her teen's little weaknesses (paranoia, weird sex partners), she hired Seneca, the most prestigious philosopher of the day, to work with him. His common-sense ethics kept the boy's dark side in check for some while. Finally, however, Nero got peevish about Agrippina's behind-the-throne bullying and brains and got the backbone to cut the umbilical cord.

Isolated from palace power at her coastal estate in Bauli, Agrippina hunkered down to write a tell-all about her family. What a great trash paperback for the beach that must have been! The historian Tacitus ate it up, even quoting from it in his book—the only morsel now left.

Chronically fearful Nero, meanwhile, came up with a clean new scheme to murder mother: a one-way cruise in a boat with a collapsible lead ceiling. Technicians bungled the job, bopped another woman, and Agrippina swam to safety—but only temporarily. A second try on land did the trick, after which the queen mom was cremated on her own couch. Years before, when astrologers had warned that Nero would be emperor and kill his mother, Agrippina retorted, "He's welcome to kill me, as long as he becomes emperor." Cool Hand Luke had nothing on this dame, who knew that you had to pay to play.

LOCUSTA

✠ ✠ ✠ ✠ ✠

If business cards had been in vogue in Rome 2,000 years ago, one of them might have read: *Locusta's the name; poison's my game.* It was surprising how many people needed the services of a professional poisoner: nobles who'd run through their money and wanted to hurry along that inheritance from dear old auntie; men going for marriage number three who found it tough to repay the dowry of wife number two; and the Gold Card customers—emperors, empresses, next-in-lines, and other wanna-bes.

Rome had a tradition of female poisoners. At a trial in 331 B.C., twenty noble-women found guilty of killing their husbands insisted they'd been brewing a tonic. Asked to prove it by drinking the stuff in court, they did and died on the spot. Locusta, however, was no one-shot amateur. From the province of Gaul, she'd gravitated to Rome, where the action was. For years, she was on retainer for one royal or another. Being a pro had its ups and downs for Locusta: a few prison terms, a couple of death sentences, and an equal number of eleventh-hour reprieves, luckily.

Locusta's first big career break came from Empress Agrippina the Younger, who'd married her uncle Claudius and put up with him until her cherub Nero was seventeen; she then gave Locusta a call. Mushrooms, one of Claudius' favorites, were fixed on as the vehicle. Despite Locusta's worst efforts, however, the dose of 'shrooms gave the emperor the runs instead of eternity. Since pros always have a backup plan, the emperor then got a fatal dose on a feather down his throat.

The next year, Locusta's career as celebrity poisoner got another boost. Nero, now emperor, still had a teenaged royal rival named Brittanicus; it seemed only fitting that this sole survivor of Claudius should join his father in the meat locker. In a bravura move involving sleight of hand with a water glass, Locusta had little Brit taken out at dinner, right in front of his family, friends, and his official food-taster. Nero was so thrilled with the results that he gave Locusta choice real estate and referred clients to her. He also awarded her a full pardon for her prior poisonings, a few of which were still on the books. Ever the entrepreneur, she launched a select school for poisoners, whose "graduates" went on to pharmaceutical successes. (Locusta was rumored to have caused more than 10,000 deaths, but that may have been advertising puffery.)

In A.D. 68, a fed-up Roman Senate issued an order to have Nero killed "the old-fashioned way," that is, stripped naked and beaten to death with rods. Even though Nero always kept a box of Locusta's finest at his bedside for such eventualities, he was forced to kill himself in a most inartistic way—with a dagger. But all bad things, not just Nero, must come to an end; that year proved lethal for Locusta too. In the brief reign of the next emperor, she and other high-profile villains were smartly marched through the city to an execution so efficient that even a pro poisoner couldn't find fault.

BOUDICCA

✣✣✣✣✣

Seldom do given names turn out to be a perfect fit; one Celtic mom in first-century A.D. Britain knew what she was doing, however. She called her little princess Boudicca, or "the victorious one," and was right on target. As things turned out, "butcher" would have worked too, but I'm getting ahead of myself.

Boudicca grew into a bodacious Brit with a river of knee-length auburn hair. She married Prasutagus, king of the Iceni tribe, who ruled the turf around present-day East Anglia, England. Early in her marriage, the Iceni tangled with the Romans, but the really bad news began about A.D. 59. Pras died, leaving half his land and wealth to his two daughters and the other half to Emperor Nero. The inheritance was a buy-off, an odious custom started by Roman emperors to refill the coffers they had blown on other stuff, such as perfume or dinner parties. The bribe didn't work. The Roman governor of the island grabbed the Iceni land anyway, flogged Queen Boudicca, and raped her two daughters for bad measure.

Everyone knows you shouldn't trifle with a redhead, especially a six-foot mother who's just been on the wrong end of a cat-o'-nine-tails. In a twinkling, Boudicca threw on her designer battle gear—a multicolored tunic, twisted gold necklace, and matching spear—and rallied nearly 100,000 flaming mad Celts, many of them women, from tribes around eastern England. Heading up the horde in her war-chariot equipped with scythe blades on the hubcaps, Boudicca charged into battle. Starting at present-day Colchester, she methodically worked her way south, killing citizens in a variety of ugly and painful ways, then torching the towns as they passed through. Next she wiped out Londinium's 20,000 inhabitants (the ashes from her bonfire can be seen in London today). By Boudicca's lights, her body count of some 70,000 Romans was no more than justifiable massacre.

Only after her army reached the Midlands did fresh Roman troops stop her furious advance. (Some had been busy fighting other frenzied females in the Druid stronghold of Mona.) Although they outnumbered the Roman troops four to one, Boudicca's Brits got out-strategized and slaughtered. The queen (and her daughters—whose names we still don't know) took poison before Romans could lay a hand on them again. Her rebellious feat had positive short-term consequences for the remaining Brits. A fact-finding commission in Rome hastily instituted a more humane policy on the island; ironically, the new soft-sell brought about the Romanization of the Iceni and other tribes far more quickly than the iron-hand rule had.

Born a slave in the emperor's household on the isle of Capri, **Dorcas** got the nod from Tiberius' imperious mother, **Livia**; with dizzying speed, she was on her way to Rome to become an ornatrix to the stars. Empress Livia must have loved her do by Dorcas; if not, this hair whiz wouldn't have lasted a week. Known as the biggest behind-the-scenes bopper in Roman politics, long-lived Livia had a knack for shortening others' life spans, from clumsy servants to family members who happened to stand in the way of her plans. Dorcas must have made decent tips—or had something on Livia, for she got freed and married a polling-clerk named Lycastus, a decent fellow who cherished her and later bragged about her abilities on her tombstone. Livia made out, too, getting goddess status a few short years after her death, despite the unseemly number of untimely exits she chalked up.

POPPAEA SABINA

✣ ✣ ✣ ✣ ✣

If there'd been a daily newspaper in little old Pompeii, its headline in A.D. 62 would have read, "Local Girl Makes Good." Okay, so the guy Poppaea Sabina married wasn't exactly GQ material. Still, emperors are emperors. By marrying Nero, Poppy became a genuine empress and wife number two for his moussed and multichinned royal perverseness.

Poppy's lover (and possibly first husband), Otho, himself destined to be one of Rome's emperors for about ten minutes in A.D. 69, introduced the two, who really hit it off. This amber-haired rich kid and her fat fiddler shared many enthusiasms: riotous living, eastern religious cults (Poppy favored Judaism, Nero the Syrian goddess cult), astrology, and perfume. Even pre-empress, Poppy kept a hundred servants busy giving bean-meal face masks and minding her herd of five hundred asses, in whose milk—mixed with spicy scent—she bathed daily. (The glow she got from the bath was nothing compared to the punch packed by her makeup of poisonous white lead, however.) Poppy even invented a pricey face cream, which she sold to the Young and the Worthless around Rome. No mean scent freak himself, Nero regularly threw parties at which perfume or rose petals showered the guests; at one party, a rainstorm of roses asphyxiated one reveler.

It was handy being married to an emperor, even one with BO. When a quake damaged Pompeii, Poppy got Nero to chip in; later, she wheedled him into lifting the ban on local gladiatorial games. (A few years earlier, hometown fans had gotten overexcited and massacred the "away team" fans in the audience.) Local currency soon wore Poppy's face, and Nero had her hailed as "Augusta." The poems he wrote to her hair caused a stampede to the salons, where Roman women used goat fat, dung, and ash to get her golden-girl look.

Pregnant when they married, Poppy gave birth to baby Claudia in January A.D. 63. Ecstatic Nero hardly bothered to persecute anyone for months—until the infant died; then he mourned by proclaiming Claudia a goddess. An artist in his own mind, Nero now focused on his singing and chariot-driving "careers," competing in the Olympics and inventing the Neronian Games after himself. Right after his Games triumph, a newly pregnant Poppy had the gall to get on his case for coming home late from the chariot races, and Nero kicked her in the stomach. Oops. One gorgeous wife dead of abuse at twenty-two. Nero promptly had her deified and burned a year's supply of Arabian spices at her funeral. Perhaps that Pompeiian headline should have read: "Local Girl Makes Divine Empress."

Though lawyers didn't get much respect in Julius Caesar's time, the silver-tongued and sassy antics of **Gaia Afrania** were far more outrage-worthy. Like other educated Romans, she took relish in suing the togas off others. The horror was, she acted as her own attorney—and quite effectively, too, judging by the hackles she raised. No one said the word "bitch" (she was, after all, the wife of a senator) but, a century later, one gutsy detractor came close: "By constantly plaguing the tribunals with such barking as the Forum had seldom heard, Gaia became the best-known example of women's litigiousness." He then said her name was a synonym for "low female morals"—quite a logic leap, even for a lawyer!

EUMACHIA

✥ ✥ ✥ ✥ ✥

One of Pompeii's leading overachievers, Eumachia came from new wealth and put it to good use. In her day—first century A.D.—her charming and probably pungent home city of 20,000 (8,000 of them slaves) on the Bay of Naples was famed for its fine wines, onions, herbs, fish sauce, honey, raw wool, and the production and dying of finished cloth. Eumachia's family had grown rich making bricks. She in turn married a man who owned acreage on the fertile slopes of Vesuvius, where they raised sheep, garden produce, and at least one boy-child.

In A.D. 62, when a major earthquake damaged many public structures, Eumachia stepped in and paid for the construction of what became one of the biggest buildings in the city. Located in the Forum at city center, her colonnaded building complex housed the wool market and served as the headquarters for the most important trade association in town—the fullers. Besides cleaning garments, fullers soaked and pressed the newly woven, bulky wool, turning it into fine cloth. By her civic generosity, Eumachia instantly shot to the top of the popularity charts with the fuller's association, which set up a statue and an inscription to her (and, I would hope, gave her free dry-cleaning for life).

Eumachia may have had an ulterior motive for her largesse. Just about the time she commissioned the grandiose structure, her son, Marcus, was running for public office. It didn't hurt that mom was a public priestess of Venus, either. (Although there were temples to Isis and many other cults in Pompeii, Venus was the city's own special hometown protectress; that's why Pompeii is so chock-a-block with murals, statues, and references to the love goddess.)

Eumachia didn't leave much to chance. In a classic social-climbing gesture, she dedicated her version of Trump Towers to the current emperor, Tiberius, and his influential mother, Livia. (The dual statues of herself and the dead but divine Livia were a nice touch.)

At one point, Eumachia took time from her whirlwind round of priestly, parental, and political duties to whip up a marble tomb for herself and her household in Pompeii's best neighborhood for the dead. If she were lucky, she may have gotten a chance to occupy its equally pretentious quarters before Vesuvius blew her beautiful city and all its works into oblivion in A.D. 79.

"Truth in advertising" wasn't just Madison Avenue hype to **Julia Felix**. A well-born native of Pompeii, Julia inherited bags of money and property. Her house, filled with handsome paintings, statues, murals, marble couches, and an interior garden patio with its own monster phallus, occupied a city block. In A.D. 62, a bad quake rocked Pompeii and damaged her property. Rather than (gasp) dip into principal, Julia paid for repairs by renting part of her digs. Her ad, painted on a wall, still reads: "For rent: part of the property of Julia Felix, on a five-year renewable lease, beginning the Ides of August—public baths, brothel, tavern, and ninety shops and rooms on the upper story." Julia's rental got a lot of action. So did some of her renters, judging by one graffito: "You were an innkeeper, a pot seller, a butcher, a baker, a farmworker, a seller of bronzes, an old-clothes dealer, now you're a potter. If you put yourself to the task of licking women, you will have carried out every type of employment."

AQUILIA SEVERA

✥ ✥ ✥ ✥ ✥

As a career, chastity seems to be losing ground in our society, judging by the sagging statistics on new nuns. A couple thousand years ago, though, the coveted job of vestal virgin, held by no more than four to seven local girls at a time, was a very big deal in Rome. Since the misty beginnings of the Eternal City, vestals had the chore of tending the Sacred Fire of Vesta, goddess of the hearth. If those kids let the fire go out, an unspecified but very bad disaster would befall Rome.

Aquilia Severa, perhaps the most famous vestal of all time, started work at the age of six or so. In July A.D. 219, she and the other vestals had the fire blazing, but a major disaster hit town anyway. His name was Egalabalus. Fourteen years old, cute in a chubby way, freakishly dressed in loads of necklaces, bangles, eyepaint, and a long silk gown described by an eye witness as "a nightmare of purple-and-gold silk," he flounced into the city with a sacred black stone in tow, drawn by six white horses. He was Rome's new emperor.

One of several unforgettable scions in a wacky dynasty of mother-and-son rulers from Roman Syria, Egalabalus loved religion and left politics to his mom Julia Soaemias. Eggy, as high priest of the Syrian sun-god, wanted to introduce the Romans to their new deity without delay. So the teen emperor shucked his current wife, had the sacred fire trucked on over to his new sun-god temple, and picked Aquilia Severa for his bride—a bit like choosing Mother Teresa to play the lead in Madonna's life story. As the rotund rascal explained, "I'm marrying Aquilia so that godlike children might spring from me, the high priest, and her, the high priestess."

As luck would have it, young Eggy got terribly busy, arranging debaucheries, cross-dressing, and having affairs with charioteers, and couldn't follow through on his dynasty plans. In less than three years, Egalabalus and his mom raised the local disgust level to such an extent that they were both murdered by the Roman guard, stripped naked, dragged through the streets in another sort of parade, and thrown into the Tiber River.

Another teen emperor, Eggy's adopted son, took the throne. The black stone and sun-god worship headed back to Syria, and Aquilia—at least, theoretically—could return to vestal virgining. She was now missing a vital component, of course, but didn't no-fault insurance apply? If a vestal deliberately broke her vow of chastity, she was buried alive in a special chamber with a lamp and a brown-bag lunch of bread, milk, oil, and water. To check their vows, the high priest ran the famous "neck test" on the little vestals every 3,000 miles. As any fool knew, the thyroid gland of a virgin expands after the first act of intercourse. Aquilia's case being unusual, perhaps they gave her early retirement on the normal thirty years each vestal served. She'd certainly been through enough to try a saint.

UMMIDIA QUADRATILLA

✤ ✤ ✤ ✤ ✤

No wonder few people care to wrestle with ancient literature—pulling facts out of antifemale biases is like untangling a ball of fishline. A case in point is Ummidia Quadratilla, a woman of wealth and generosity to her hometown of Casinum. During her seventy-eight years, she laid out major cash for a temple, a stage, and an amphitheater for her city in central Italy. Clearly, Ummidia loved the theater, which in her day meant the comic, often bawdy pantomime. She also was a board-game freak. In later years, she amused herself at home with both, being rich enough to keep an entire troupe of actors on tap.

Ummidia also had the chore of raising her grandson. She often asked family friend and writer Pliny the Younger for his advice about the boy's education. Her toughest job was keeping the kid away from her low-brow but irresistible amusements; he grew up to be a quite a snob, so I guess she was able to.

When Ummidia died, she left two-thirds of her estate to her grandson and the other third to her granddaughter. In a letter to a friend, Pliny applauds her politically correct inheritance, frowns on her trivial pursuits, but grudgingly gives the old gal a bonus point for not exposing her heir to trashy "women's idle hours" activities. What does Pliny have to say about her accomplishments—raising her grandkid, supporting the arts, donating money for public works? Zilch. Fortunately, we have more than Pliny to go on; inscriptions now validate Ummidia's contributions. Just think, though, how many lives where the cookie has crumbled the other way must still lie hidden.

BASSILLA

✤ ✤ ✤ ✤ ✤

Although women had always been part of the audience for Greek theater, females didn't get to be *hypocrites* (the Greek word for "actor") until Roman times. In the lively, raunchy, sometimes gross realism of pantomime theater, actresses like Bassilla demonstrated that they had as much talent for hypocrisy as the next man. They also got to show off their flair for nudity, stunts, and cross-dressing; women also played male roles, just as men had played female parts for centuries.

Bassilla came from Aquileia, the most commercially important city in northern Italy in the third century A.D. Her acting career took her to towns and cities around the Roman world. Rank-and-file actresses, many of whom began as slaves, had the same social standing as actors: none. (A Roman law forbid senators and other freeborn men from marrying actresses and other morally dubious types.)

Bassilla and others who reached stardom became famous, wealthy, and sought-after, graciously hanging out with cultural groupies like emperors Nero and Hadrian. To reach success, Bassilla did it all: from dancing parts to acting roles in plays, mimes, and choruses. The schtick she became most famous for, however, was death. An inscription about her in the theater at Aquileia praises Bassilla for her uncanny ability to die realistically on stage and calls her "the tenth Muse."

PLOTINA

✤ ✤ ✤ ✤ ✤

When you wince in horror at old photos of yourself, ever notice how it's always the hairdo that's the disaster epicenter? Poor Plotina had the same problem: empress of the vast Roman Empire, yet captured for all time in marble and on coins as She of the Truly Weird Coiffure. Looking at the grim, gluey mop she sported, you can just hear some empress-hating hairdresser saying, "Trust me—you'll look great with a three-story cheese Danish on your head!" In spite of her dreaded locks, Plotina had depth and character. Childless, she and Emperor Trajan raised little cousin Hadrian as his successor and married him off to Plotina's liking.

A lifelong student of Epicurean philosophy, this soft-spoken steel magnolia

spent her life advising her husband—and later the next emperor—on important public and private issues. Tragically, however, her greatest influence was on high fashion; in her day, and for centuries after, women actually strove to emulate the Empress of Bad Hair. Even more tragically, a few succeeded in outdoing her. Despite her hairy faux pas, Plotina was declared divine in A.D. 121.

SABINA

✢ ✢ ✢ ✢ ✢

For six years, Sabina took part in one of the world's great love affairs; her only gripe was her role—voyeur. As empress, she got to watch the all-too-public *amore* between her fiftyish but frisky husband, Hadrian, and a pouty-lipped young stud named Antinous. How did perky, sweet Sabina get into this jam? Via auntie Plotina, the prior empress, whose match-making stuck her with an unenthused Hadrian. Theirs was a superglue marriage, however, stuck together for three decades, during which Sabina's supply of charm and cheerfulness congealed into bad temper. In her loneliness, Sabina did the most spiteful thing she could think of: remain childless—no mean trick in her day, when abstinence, anal sex, or abortion were the only guarantees.

Despite mutual detestation, Sabina and the restless emperor often traveled together. In A.D. 130, Hadrian, Antinous, Sabina, and her friend Julia took a boat trip through Egypt. One night, Antinous went for a dip in the Nile and never came up. Hadrian, already ill, went nuts with grief: The party had to carry the corpse on the boat, which put a real damper on the sight-seeing. Before the cremation ashes were cold, Hadrian declared his boy-toy from the Black Sea a god—a first for a young nobody. A chain of temples to Antinous worship soon opened around the Med.

Oddly enough, everyone bought the idea that Antinous had committed suicide. Though Sabina may not have done any pushing, chances are she did some wishing. Even with Antinous off the screen, Sabina and Hadrian never clicked; they logged another seven years together before taking an eternal siesta side by side. With a marriage this tepid, death probably *warmed up* their relationship.

PRISCILLA

✣ ✣ ✣ ✣ ✣

You think it was tough being a Christian in the first century A.D.? Try being a Jew *and* a Christian, like Priscilla and her husband, Aquila. Good folks and movers extraordinaire, this couple lived among other well-to-do Jews in the fancy Aventine Hill section of Rome. They were tent-makers, an evidently more lucrative craft in their day than ours. Sometime around A.D. 40, they converted, and their digs became one of the first Christian churches in the city.

The round-robin began when Emperor Claudius expelled every activist Jew from Rome. Priscilla and Aquila packed, leaving their home for Corinth in Greece. Barely unpacked and into a new house, they offered it as a local meeting place for Christians, and who shows up but Saint Paul. An old tent-maker himself, he soon was camped out on their couch, preaching the Gospel by day and crafting a few Colemans by night. When he left for Asia Minor less than two years later, the two gypsies accompanied him. In Ephesus, they set up another church center. Five years later, riots against the Christians erupt: time to get out the trunks again. The trio returned to Rome, where they may have found their property still standing. As tent-makers, Priscilla and Aquila were the perfect couple to spread the Gospel; their astonishing travelogue of faith and generosity reveals a good deal about the spread of Christianity and the turmoil that accompanied it. Not only did Jews join the Christian Church, they soon split into groups, one Jewish Christian faction insisting on circumcision for all non-Jewish converts to their sect—a painful issue, needless to say.

BLAESILLA

✢ ✢ ✢ ✢ ✢

In A.D. 384, the death of an anorexic twenty year old named Blaesilla made news in Rome. Instead of fasting to fit a size five or because of "poor self-image," Blaesilla starved herself for Jesus and Jerome—not necessarily in that order. An early Christian writer, teacher, translator, and anal retentive, Jerome wasn't merely anti-sex or anti-marriage, he was anti-body. Like other church members, he expected the Second Coming any minute, which would make meals, bathing, and illness irrelevant anyway.

Blaesilla wasn't alone in her zeal for the ultimate slim fast; her widowed mother, Paula, and sister, Eustochium, also fasted and prayed tirelessly. Paula had need of Christian forbearance after Blaesilla's death.

Instead of professing sorrow for his role in encouraging such extremes, Jerome blasted the bereft mom for her "detestable, sacrilegious tears," saying that Satan was totally mortified at Blaesilla's triumphant ascent to heaven, and Paula should buck up. When Blaesilla's mother and sister stopped their babyish crying, they accompanied Jerome to Bethlehem, where they helped him edit his Latin translation of the Bible for thirty-five years—without credit, of course. Paula, determined to use the family wealth for charitable works to serve the church, managed to achieve the ultimate deficit philanthropy. At her death in A.D. 404, she left career virgin Eustochium with an amazing debt; however, she and Eusty did go on to sainthood, so perhaps it was all worthwhile.

ETHERIA

✤ ✤ ✤ ✤ ✤

A strange combination of derring-do and deadly dull, Etheria wandered the world when it took real guts to do so. Guts *and* time, lots of it: The best speed human travelers could hope for on land with roads was twenty to forty miles per day. On the sea, it took a minimum of a month to sail from Spain to Syria. Etheria's three-year religious journey, from the Spanish end of the Mediterranean basin to the Holy Land at the other, took place a century after Christianity had been declared one of the official religions of the empire in A.D. 313. Speculation has it that Etheria must have been born in comfortable circumstances in Spain or France; how else would she have had the funds to carry out such a trip? Etheria clearly had a spirit both austere and adventurous—pious enough to make her become a nun in the first place, and macho enough to tackle such a rugged pilgrimage, alone, on foot, donkey, or camelback, through lands filled with bandits, bad weather, rotten water, and worse bugs.

This intrepid nun didn't miss a thing. She covered much of Palestine, Asia Minor, and Syria; she saw Egypt and the Nile; she hit every holy site in Jerusalem and every rock up and down Mt. Sinai, including the provocatively named Graves of Lust in the valley. She made a three-day side trip to the shrine of Saint Thecla, and got as far north as the shores of the Black Sea and the capital of Constantinople. And this is only what we *know* of her itinerary—her diary, written in Latin, is still missing two-thirds of its pages.

The only downer to Etheria's delightful vagabonding is her incredibly pro-saic description of it all, directed at her sister nuns. Reading her journal is like watching the slide show from hell, the slow-mo travel chat you get dragged to by your spouse, where every out-of-focus photo makes you want to scream: Why didn't you point the camera over there, show us the real stuff, give us the telling detail? Etheria seemed determined to link every spot with a biblical reference, no matter how obscure—most of which are described in the most amazingly color-less fashion. The people she must have seen, the foreign smells, the sunrises, the birdsong—none are recorded or perhaps deemed worthy of interest. And what about the disasters, without which no trip—especially a three-year one—is com-plete? Not one word.

One thing Etheria didn't have to worry about in her travels was the vagabond's perennial search for a clean bed and bath. Early Christian nuns and monks made a fetish of filth. Cleanliness was not next to godliness—far from it. One female visitor to Jerusalem boasted that she hadn't washed her face in eighteen years, so as not to disturb the holy water used at her baptism; she and Etheria probably had a lot in common.

FABIOLA

✣ ✣ ✣ ✣ ✣

As Jesus had done nearly four hundred years earlier, Fabiola focused her attention and love on the invisible people of her world: the poor, the humble, and the suffering. This upper-crust offspring of a distinguished Roman family converted to Christianity at age twenty but quickly struck out twice in the love and marriage department, first marrying a man so debauched that she got a civil divorce from him, then living in sin with another fellow, an action that so scandalized her Christian group that they threw her out. Luckily, both men expired soon thereafter, and her church group let the instantly more respectable widow Fabiola return after some public penance.

A good thing, too, because Fabiola single-handedly was to do more for public health, medicine, and Christianity than half a hundred of her contemporaries. She took her big bucks to Bethlehem, hoping to join in the good works of Christian leader and scholar Jerome and his band of wealthy women activists, who were busy translating the Bible into Latin. Their activities, however, just didn't seem lively enough for the likes of Fabiola. About this time, the Huns started terrorizing Palestine, promising action of a more dire sort, so Fabiola fled the Holy Land, Jerome and group hot on her heels, and returned to Rome.

There, in Rome's port city of Ostia, with the help of Pammachius, a Christian monk and philanthropist, Fabiola established a large free public hospital, the world's first. To carry out the hospital's mission, she recruited a dozen other well-to-do Roman matrons, who contributed funds and labored as nurses and physicians. Not only did her facility revolutionize health service, which at that time meant either military or private care, it made her famous. No squeamishness about this lady—Fabiola went right out and collected poor patients off the streets. Jerome was truly in awe of her. He called her "the glory of the Church, the astonishment of the Gentiles, the mother of the poor, and the consolation of the saints." In one of his letters, he really got into the wretchedness of the beings she so tenderly rescued: "they have leprous arms, swollen bellies, shrunken thighs, dropsical legs. . . their flesh gnawed and rotten and squirming with little worms. . . ." Besides charity and a strong stomach, this grand woman had energy to spare; a traveler herself, she also founded a travelers' hostel at Porto Romano. She was busy planning other enterprises abroad when death caught her by surprise in A.D. 399. All of Rome turned out for her funeral; a grateful Church later declared Fabiola a saint.

Where did the elite and the tacky meet in first-century A.D. Italy? The public baths, where men and women came daily for exercise (bladder-ball and fencing were favorites), massage, snacks, and social intercourse—and, from time to time, intercourse of another sort. Thanks to bath graffiti in Herculaneum (the other city buried by Vesuvius) we know quite a bit about the party animals who made the area such a fun place—**Primigenia** from nearby Nuceria, for instance. Like other hookers, Primigenia advertised in the Italian Yellow Pages: She wrote her name, address, and price on a wall in the Street of Venus. Primi had more admirers than dogs have dandruff. Fans wrote of her charms on walls, in baths—even on tombstones. On the day Vesuvius blew its top, she and a middle-aged banker named Hermeros had a date. His note calling her "conqueror of hearts" still adorns the bathhouse. Let's hope they got to party hearty before the really Big Bang.

JUSTA HONORIA

✛ ✛ ✛ ✛ ✛

No one left a likeness of Attila the Hun, one of the world's truly great bad guys, but we do have a portrait on a Roman coin of his honey. Strange as it sounds, the Scourge of God had a girlfriend named Justa Grata Honoria, and not just any lowlife Hun-happy hot mama either—Justa was the sister of Valentinian Three, emperor of the western half of the Roman Empire.

On second thought, maybe Justa was just a tad wild; unmarried, supposed to be devoted to Christian celibacy, she managed to get a wee bit knocked up in A.D. 434. Attila wasn't in the picture yet; the proud father was a commoner, her farm manager. Everyone at the imperial court in Ravenna, including her brother, thought Justa planned a run at the emperorship. (After all, her female relatives had taken major roles in ruling the empire during their empress stints.) So big brother grounded Justa in a big way, banishing her to the court of family member Theodosius Two in Constantinople, the eastern half of the empire. For good measure, he gave Justa's lover—and possibly the baby—a permanent time-out. When Justa was finally allowed to return to Italy, bossy brother then signed her up to marry someone safe, a guy with good family but no tiresome ambitions of any sort.

Wily Justa managed to put those wedding bells on perennial hold; she had her own plans for the future. Happily, big brother Val hadn't fired any of her personal servants yet, so she sent one of her eunuchs to boldly go where no one had gone—to the camp of Attila the Hun, who was currently chewing on the weakening edges of the Roman Empire. The eunuch carried Justa's ring and a mushy note, saying how fabulous she thought he was, and would he be interested in a spot of revenge—for a generous fee, of course. An old romantic at heart, Attila fired back an okay and an offer of marriage. Inevitably, brother Val got wind of this and tried to break up the pen pals by telling Attila: "My sister's taken and, besides, she doesn't have any rights to the throne, anyway—so get lost."

Never a barbarian to take "Hell no!" for an answer, Attila invaded Gaul to show his feelings, later showing up in Italy to claim his unlikely fiancée. Italy not having a SWAT team at that time, Pope Leo jumped in to negotiate with the number one Hun and keep him from burning Rome to the ground. Providence only knows what might have happened if spitfire Justa had gotten to gallop off with Attila. Fate, however, called Attila's Quick-Pik number, and he died in A.D. 453, before this odd couple could forge a relationship or even wreak a little mean-spirited revenge.

In Roman times, painters painted for lofty motives. It certainly wasn't for money (lousy in most cases) or recognition (most painters didn't even get to sign their work, being lumped as artisans). **Iaia** broke the mold. From Cyzicus (now Turkey) on the Sea of Marmora, she spent her life in Rome, specializing in portrait oil painting and ivory engraving. Unmarried and with no NEA grants, Iaia made it on merit; she had such a following that her work sold for higher prices than her two best-known male contemporaries. Iaia was also famous as Rome's fastest-draw artist, a blessing when you work on commissions. A century after her death, this artistic success story still got kudos for her self-portrait and character studies.

SELECTED BIBLIOGRAPHY

Because the information about ancient women is thinly scattered through a vast body of material, space doesn't permit more than a brief mention of useful sources. The core material for this book comes from a twenty-year winnowing of the ancient writers, Greek and Roman. Most appear in one of three series: the Harvard Loeb Library, the Penguin Classics, and the Modern Library. The most useful authors are Athenaeus, Diogenes Laertius, Diodorus Siculus, Herodotus, Josephus, Pausanias, Pliny, Plutarch, Strabo, Suetonius, and Tacitus.

Other core material comes from nonliterary sources, such as collections of inscriptions, decrees, and papyri documents; books on ancient coins; archaeological reports; doctoral theses; and documents from Mesopotamian, Egyptian, Greek, Roman, and early Christian times that contain letters, lists, and diaries. The publishers of the Thames and Hudson and the Time/Life series on the ancient world also issue many worthy books.

Other recommendations:

Balsdon, J. P. V. D. *Roman Women.* John Day, 1963.

Batto, Bernard. *Studies on Women at Mari.* Johns Hopkins University Press, 1974.

Bloom, Harold, et al. *The Book of J.* Grove Weidenfeld, 1990.

Boccaccio, Giovanni. *Concerning Famous Women.* Rutgers University Press, 1963.

Boulding, Elise. *The Underside of History,* vol. 1. Sage Publishers, 1992.

Dalley, Stephanie. *Mari and Karana.* Longman, 1984.

Fantham, Elaine, et al, eds. *Women in the Classical World.* Oxford University Press, 1994.

Fraser, Antonia. *The Warrior Queens.* Vintage Press, 1988.

Fremantle, Anne. *Treasury of Early Christianity.* North American Library, 1953.

Herm, Gerhard. *The Phoenicians.* Morrow, 1975.

Hirshfield, Jane, ed. *Women in Praise of the Sacred.* HarperCollins, 1994.

Holum, Kenneth. *Theodosian Empresses.* University of California Press, 1982.

James, Peter, et al. *Ancient Inventions*. Ballantine, 1994.

Keuls, Eva. *The Reign of the Phallus*. Harper & Row, 1985.

Klingaman, William. *The First Century*. HarperCollins, 1986.

Kraemer, Ross, ed. *Maenads, Martyrs, Matrons, Monastics*. Fortress Press, 1988.

Kramer, Samuel. *The Sumerians*. University of Chicago Press, 1963.

Lehmann, Johannes. *The Hittites*. Viking, 1975.

Macurdy, Helen. *Hellenistic Queens*. ARES Press, 1985.

Oates, Joan. *Babylon*. Thames & Hudson, 1979.

Pomerey, Sarah. *Women in Hellenistic Egypt*. Wayne State University Press, 1990.

Renault, Mary. *The Nature of Alexander*. Pantheon, 1975.

Seibert, Ilse. *Women in the Ancient Near East*. Schram, 1974.

Snyder, Jane M. *The Woman and the Lyre*. Southern Illinois University Press, 1989.

Vandenberg, Philipp. *Mystery of the Oracles*. Macmillan, 1982.

Yadin, Yigael. *Bar-Kokhba*. Random House, 1971.

INDEX

VICKI LEÓN

Vicki León, afflicted with an incurable itch about the doings of women in ancient times, has prowled the Mediterranean, ferreted out facts from archaeological reports, and delved into the dimmest depths of library archives for her material. This vast heap of data joins her mountains of other material gathered while writing 13 earlier books on nature and travel.

WILD WOMAN ASSOCIATION

In 1992, with the publication of *Wild Women* by Autumn Stephens, Conari Press founded in the Wild Woman Association. Today there are over 3,000 card-carrying Wild Women in cities throughout the world—and some even meet regularly with their untamed and uproarious sisters in an effort to encourage wildness. The Association's primary purpose is to rediscover and rewrite our wild foresisters back into history . . . and if there is a wild woman in *your* family we hope you might help by sending us information for possible inclusion in subsequent volumes of the *Wild Women* series.

To receive your free membership card and the Wild Woman Association Newsletter, please mail this page to:

The Wild Woman Association
2550 Ninth Street, Suite 101
Berkeley, CA 94710

Let's rewrite history with women in it!

Conari Press, established in 1987, publishes books on topics ranging from spirituality and women's history to sexuality and personal growth. Our main goal is to publish quality books that will make a difference in people's lives—both how we feel about ourselves and how we relate to one another. All of our books are available in bookstores everywhere.

Our readers are our most important resource, and we value your input, suggestions, and ideas. We'd love to hear from you—after all, we are publishing books for you!

For a complete catalog or to get on our mailing list, please contact us at:

CONARI PRESS

2550 Ninth Street, Suite 101
Berkeley, California 94710
800-685-9595